THE ART OF ROYAL ICING

THE ART OF ROYAL ICING

by

AUDREY HOLDING

Glossop Centre for Educational and Recreational Activities, Derbyshire, UK

Illustrated by

John Holding

APPLIED SCIENCE PUBLISHERS LTD
LONDON

APPLIED SCIENCE PUBLISHERS LTD
RIPPLE ROAD, BARKING, ESSEX, ENGLAND

British Library Cataloguing in Publication Data

Holding, Audrey
The art of royal icing.
1. Icings, Cake
I. Title
641.8′653 TX771

ISBN 0-85334-860-X

WITH 164 ILLUSTRATIONS

First Edition 1980
Reprinted 1983

Printed in Great Britain by Galliard (Printers) Ltd, Great Yarmouth

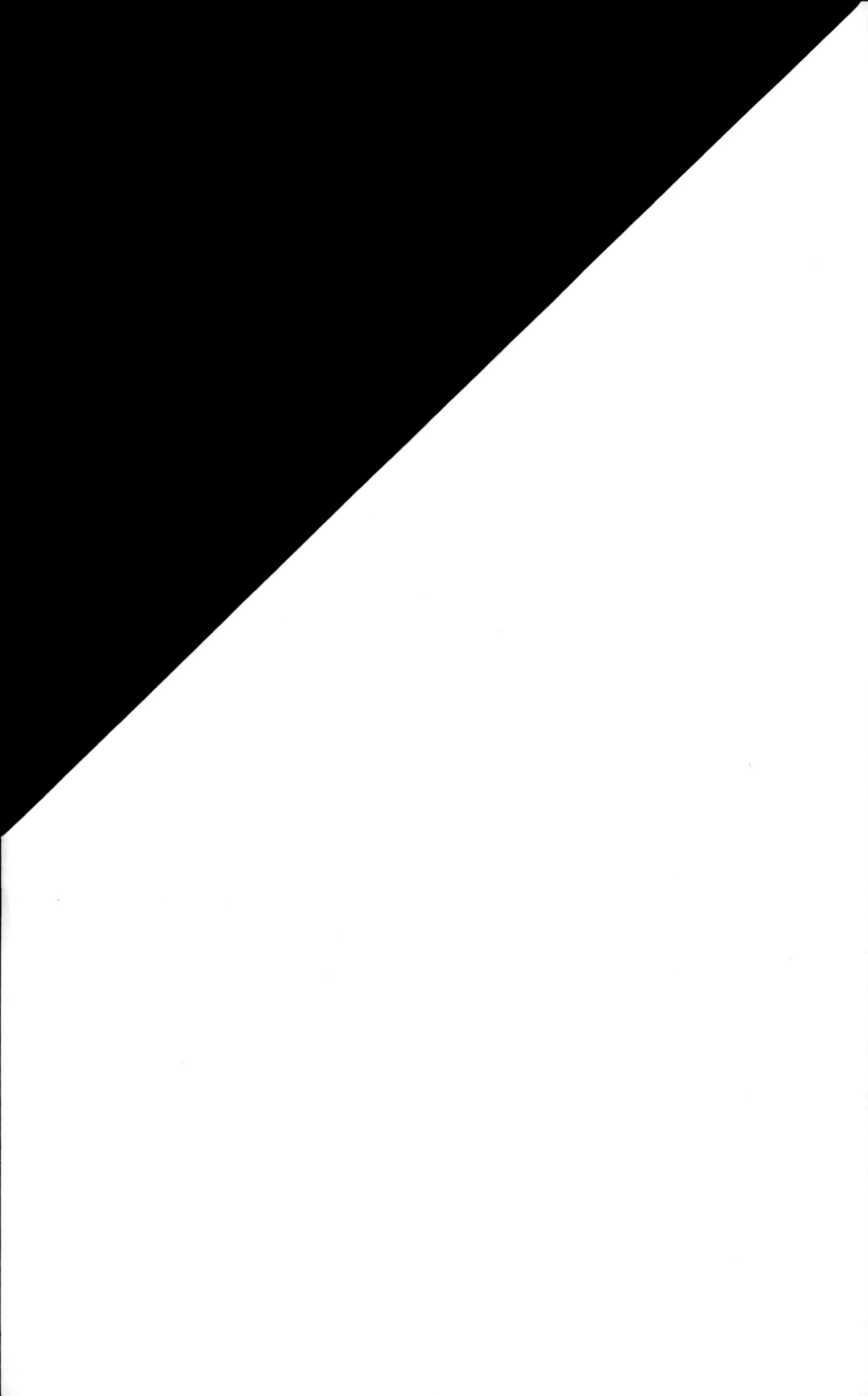

Acknowledgements

The author would like to thank the following for their co-operation:

Sadie Bruckshaw, Paul Walker, Arthur L. Jones,
Dr. Willis Elwood, Roger Gibson,
Frank Dearnley, St. David's College, Llandudno,
Audrey Tarrant, The Medici Society,
The Gordon Fraser Gallery Ltd,
Hallmark Cards Inc.,
Donkey Breed Society, and
Joint Charity Cards Associates Ltd.

Foreword

It is with great pleasure that I write the foreword to this excellent book on royal icing work. Audrey Holding has been a dedicated cake decorator for many years. Originally taken up as a hobby, she decided in 1971 to pursue this art further by studying at Hollings College, Manchester for the coveted City & Guilds Certificate in Design and Decoration of Flour Confectionery which she obtained with a Credit.

Since then she has lectured at Tameside Bakery College in vocational and non-vocational subjects and is teaching at an Adult Educational Centre in Derbyshire where her gift is very much appreciated by all who come in contact with her. Viewers of B.B.C. Television in the North West were recently privileged to watch her demonstrate her skills with Stuart Hall in the 'Look North' programme.

This book will, I am sure, be of great value not only to the novice in the art of royal icing but also to those who have had experience. Her enthusiasm is infectious!

JUNE ELWOOD, M. INST. B.B., M.C.F.A.,
Cake Artistry Studio,
Worsley,
Manchester.

Preface

The aim of this book is three-fold; to explain the craft to those who have had no previous knowledge of the subject; to extend the knowledge of those who already practise the art, whether as a profession or as a hobby; and finally to point out that the art of royal icing, like every other art, depends very much on the individual choice. What one person will like, another will not, and the emphasis in this book will be on edibility. Plastic flowers, bells, paper leaves and the like are, to me, unacceptable on a cake and I shall explain how to avoid the use of such artificial decorations.

This book does not set out to replace practical lessons. In fact those who have had no previous experience of the subject will, I hope, want to further their knowledge. Local evening schools and technical colleges will be able to help in this respect. However, do find out before enrolling exactly what the course entails and so avoid wasting time and money should it not come up to expectations. No two teachers are alike so be prepared to learn new ways of doing almost everything! Only by doing this can an individual style be developed and thus establish a personal 'trade mark'.

In this little book I have tried to open up for you something of the delights of the art of cake decorating and to explain in a straightforward manner the basic techniques.

I can only hope that your enthusiasm will be fired and what you will derive as much pleasure as I have done from creative activity with these simple, edible decorations.

AUDREY HOLDING

Contents

Illustrations

Chapter 1

Equipment

With the exception of a turntable and piping tubes, most equipment required for royal icing can be found in any kitchen. However, as they must be kept absolutely grease-free these items should, if possible, be used only for royal icing. This is not absolutely essential with bowls and metal knives as these can be washed in boiling-hot water, but the wooden spoon or spatula should not be used for anything else. The reason for this is that grease prevents aeration of the sugar and also causes the icing to discolour.

I do appreciate that for those not connected with the bakery trade some items might be difficult to acquire. Those already attending classes will find that most teachers are able to obtain equipment for them. For the rest it can be rather a frustrating business! However, it is possible and there are a few companies that provide a mail order service for every possible piece of equipment from colouring to cake stands.

The turntable shown on the right in Fig. 1 is the one normally used for royal icing; it is ideal, being heavy and strong. However, for those who are taking up icing as a hobby and feel unable to buy this expensive type, the one on the left is quite satisfactory. Though it is much lighter I have found it quite adequate in my classes and it costs less than a quarter of the price. It is sold as a demonstration turntable for flower arranging and I suggest your local florist might be able to assist in obtaining one.

Only one bowl or basin is usually required, and, as mentioned before, it can be used for other things providing it is absolutely clean and grease-free before being used for icing. I find that glazed earthenware or glass is best; polythene ones tend not to be quite so rigid when mixing. However, polythene ones with air-tight lids are ideal for storing ready-mixed icing (Fig. 2).

Fig. 1. Turntables.

Fig. 2. Bowls.

It is essential to have a measuring jug if using powdered albumen (see later), as this has to be reconstituted. Powdered albumen has to be weighed so the scale tray as well as the measuring jug must be grease-free before use (Fig. 3).

Two palette knives are necessary and both should be stainless steel. The smaller one with a 10-cm (4-in) blade is used for filling paper bags and coating the sides of a cake with icing. The larger one has a 15-cm (6-in)

Fig. 3. Measuring jug.

blade and is mainly used for paddling down the icing on top of the cake (Fig. 4).

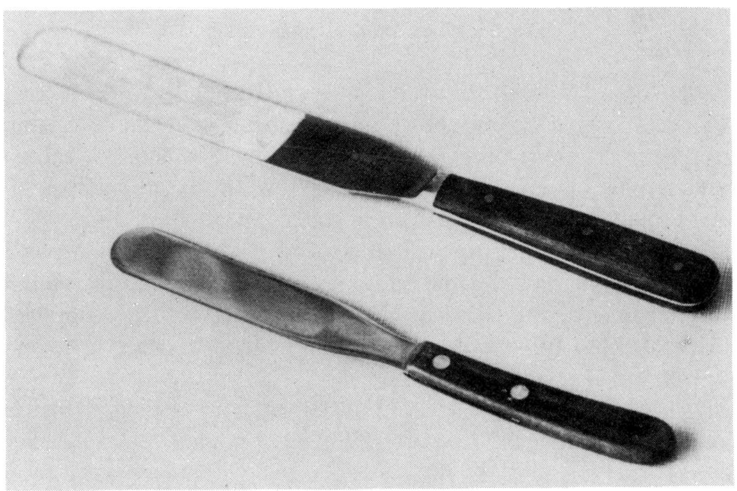

Fig. 4. Palette knives.

You will need a rule (often referred to as a 'straight-edge') to obtain a smooth finish on the top of the cake. The one on the left in Fig. 5 is made from stainless steel and is preferable to the one on the right which is wood. The wooden one is a piece of beading obtained from any joiner for next to no cost at all. It is important that the edge is well sand-papered to ensure smoothness. The stainless steel strip can be bought or made, but again there must be no rough edges, otherwise marks will appear on the top of the cake. Plastic ones are also available, but I find they are too flexible for this purpose.

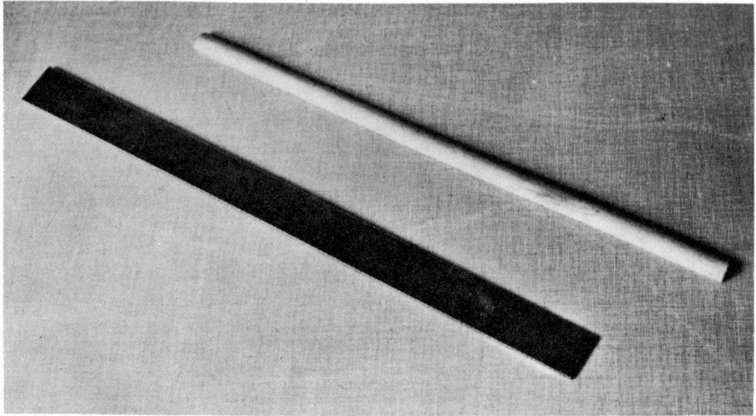

Fig. 5. Metal and wooden rules.

The side scraper is used for obtaining a smooth finish to the side of the cake. Plastic ones like the one shown on the left in Fig. 6 can be bought and are very cheap. The one on the right is made out of stainless steel, and is preferable as there is no tendency for it to bend. Both are suitable, but as with the straight-edge, they must be absolutely smooth.

I prefer to use a spatula rather than a wooden spoon for mixing royal icing. A spatula is easier to handle and does not trap air, causing bubbles in the icing, so much as a wooden spoon. However, both are suitable and inexpensive to buy. Whichever is chosen, remember to keep it exclusively for use with royal icing (Fig. 7).

Figure 8 shows only one type of tube as, in my opinion, this is far superior to any other that I have used. They are made of solid nickel-silver and are easily obtainable by those connected with the bakery trade or through evening schools and colleges. If difficulty is experienced in getting this type of tube, I suggest you buy only those of a similar shape. The type

Fig. 6. Side scrapers.

Fig. 7. Wooden spoon and spatula.

made to screw into a piping syringe is not suitable for using with a paper bag.

The numbers of the tubes in Fig. 8 are 13 and 44 star, and 3, 2, 1 and 0 plain.

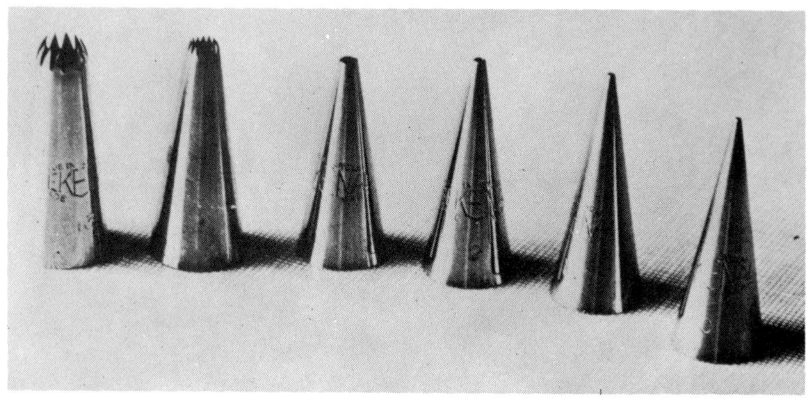

Fig. 8. Piping tubes.

Other equipment required is as follows:

A fine paint brush for washing tubes and for many other uses which will be explained later.
Greaseproof paper for bag making.
A fine mesh sieve (wire or nylon).
Cocktail sticks.
Edible colourings.
Scissors.
Dish cloths.
A damp tea towel for covering the bowl of icing.
Fine sandpaper.
Waxed paper for runout work.

Chapter 2

The Fruit Cake and Almond Paste or Marzipan

Making the Cake

Before getting down to the more interesting part of actually icing the cake, we must first consider the cake itself. Most people have their own favourite recipe for a rich fruit cake, and it is often because they can make a good cake that they develop an interest in royal icing.

Here is a recipe that I use. I quite appreciate that people in the trade would not use such small quantities, but this recipe is aimed at the beginner who is likely to be making only one cake.

225 g (8 oz) plain flour.
Half teaspoonful ground cinnamon.
Half teaspoonful ground mixed spice.
Half teaspoonful ground mace.
225 g (8 oz) butter.
225 g (8 oz) dark soft brown sugar.
4 large eggs, beaten.
The grated rind of one lemon.
225 g (8 oz) currants.
225 g (8 oz) seedless raisins.
225 g (8 oz) sultanas.
100 g (4 oz) glacé cherries, halved.
75 g (3 oz) mixed chopped peel.
75 g (3 oz) nibbed almonds.
2–3 tablespoonful brandy.

Method: Grease and line the cake tin. Sift the flour and spices together. Beat the butter and sugar until creamy, then gradually add the beaten eggs.

Fold in the flour alternately with the mixed fruit, nuts and lemon rind. Finally stir in the brandy. Bake at 120° C (250° F) or gas mark ½ for 3–4 h, according to the size of tin. For increased quantities the cooking time would have to be adjusted.

This quantity (225 g flour) is sufficient for the following:

A 15-cm (6-in) square and a 15-cm (6-in) round tin, or
a 20-cm (8-in) square tin, or
a 23-cm (9-in) round tin.

One and a half times this quantity, 350 g (12 oz), is sufficient for the following:

A 18-cm (7-in) square and a 20-cm (8-in) round tin, or
a 23-cm (9-in) square tin, or
a 25-cm (10-in) round tin.

Double the quantity, 450 g (1 lb), is sufficient for:

A 15-cm (6-in) round and a 25-cm (10-in) square tin, or
a 28-cm (11-in) square tin.

Treble the quantity, 680 g (1½ lb), is sufficient for:

A 30-cm (12-in) square tin.

ALMOND PASTE OR MARZIPAN

Some people think that almond paste and marzipan are exactly the same, but this is not true. Although both contain almonds and sugar, almond paste is easily made in the home whilst marzipan is a manufactured paste.

Both are suitable as a base for royal icing. Almond paste tends to be softer and a little gritty. Marzipan is a firmer paste and very smooth.

I prefer to use marzipan, especially on wedding cakes, rather than make almond paste. There are two types available; one is golden in colour whilst the other is off-white. The latter is preferable since, if it is used for modelling, any colour may be added and a correct colour obtained. Also, this 'natural' marzipan is unlikely to cause any staining on the icing which happens when almond paste or marzipan have been handled too long. Whichever is used, always keep the paste well-wrapped in plastic kitchen wrapping to exclude any air and so avoid the formation of a crust.

The natural marzipan is much more difficult to find in the shops than the golden type, but it is available. It is usually Danish and sold in small rolls rather than the usual rectangular blocks (Fig. 9).

Fig. 9. Marzipan

MAKING ALMOND PASTE

Almond paste is expensive, so do not make more than required. As a guide, after weighing the baked cake, half of the weight will be required in almond paste or marzipan.

For those who wish to make almond paste, here is the recipe:

225 g (8 oz) icing sugar.
225 g (8 oz) caster sugar.
225 g (8 oz) ground almonds.
Enough whole eggs (1–2) or egg yolks to make a firm paste.

Method: Sieve together all the dry ingredients. Bind to a firm paste with the egg. A little rum may be added to give extra flavour. Be careful not to knead the mixture and therefore express the oil from the almonds which would cause staining on the finished cake. Wrap immediately to prevent the paste from crusting.

This mixture will weigh just over 675 g ($1\frac{1}{2}$ lb) and is enough to cover the top and sides of a 1·36-kg (3 lb) fruit cake baked in a 18–20-cm (7–8-in) tin.

Covering the Cake with Almond Paste or Marzipan

Before commencing to cover the cake, have ready to hand a deep silver cake board at least 50 mm (2-in) larger than the cake itself.

Boiled apricot purée will also be required to be applied to the surface of the cake prior to covering it with paste. The purée is not applied merely to stick the paste on to the cake, but to form an essential seal preventing fermentation taking place. This is why it must be applied boiling hot.

Difficulty may arise in buying the purée, but it can be made easily as follows:

Apricot purée: Empty one jar of apricot jam into a saucepan. Add four tablespoons of water, the juice of one lemon, and slowly bring to the boil. Boil gently for 5 min, sieve, discard any skins, and boil again for a further 5 min. Place in a clean jar and cover. Larger quantities can be made and kept until required.

COVERING THE TOP

Having the cake, the paste, the board and the purée we can commence to cover the cake. The procedure is the same for either almond paste or marzipan, and either square or round cakes.

1. Make sure that, in addition to icing sugar, the following equipment is to hand: Turntable, rolling pin, palette knife, short ruler, tape measure, and a small sharp knife for trimming paste.
2. Choose a clean work surface and check that the top of the cake is level; if not, trim with a sharp knife. In some cases it may be preferable to turn the cake over and use the flat bottom as the top to give a more even surface on which to apply the paste.
3. Bring a pan of purée slowly to the boil.
4. Sprinkle the working surface with a light dusting of icing sugar to prevent the paste from sticking.
5. Roll out approximately two thirds of the paste into a piece slightly larger than the top of the cake. This ensures a thick covering on the top of the cake and a very thin one on the side.
6. Take the cake to the pan of boiling purée and with the use of a palette knife thinly spread the surface of the cake with purée.
7. After making sure that the paste has not stuck to the working surface, press the cake, puréed surface down, on to the paste and trim away any surplus paste with a sharp knife (Fig. 10).
8. Press the paste to the side of the cake using a palette knife.
9. Turn cake the right way up and place in the centre of the silver board (Fig. 11).

COVERING THE SIDES

Round Cake

1. Make sure the work surface is perfectly clean and free from any cake crumbs. Dust with a little icing sugar.
2. Measure the circumference of the cake with a tape measure and the depth with a ruler (Figs. 12 and 13).

Fig. 10. Trimming paste from the top of the cake.

Fig. 11. Cake placed on board.

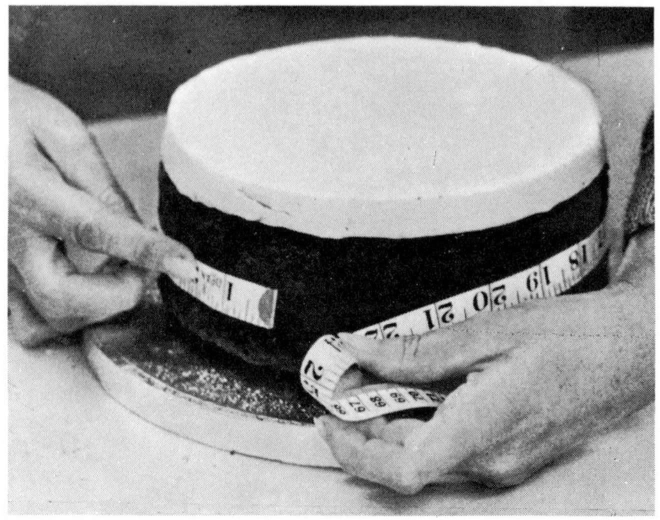

Fig. 12. Tape measure around the side of the cake.

Fig. 13. Ruler on the side of the cake.

3. Form the remaining paste into a sausage shape and roll out to a thin 4-mm ($\frac{1}{8}$-in) strip, the length required to go round the cake. Trim both top and bottom of this strip to the exact depth of the cake as measured with the ruler (Fig. 14).

Fig. 14. Strip of paste for the side of the cake.

4. Roll up this strip like a bandage (Fig. 15).
5. Spread the side of the cake with boiling purée (Fig. 16).
6. Place the cake, still on the board, on the turntable. Being careful not to stretch the paste, gently unroll the paste round the cake, taking care not to overlap where the paste meets (Fig. 17).

Square Cake

With a square cake the procedure is similar to the above, but to ensure that square corners are maintained, individual strips of paste are fitted to each side in turn (Fig. 18).

If slightly rounded corners are preferred, then the procedure is exactly the same as for a round cake. It is not absolutely essential that the side strip

Fig. 15. Rolling a bandage of paste.

Fig. 16. Spreading the side of the cake with purée.

Fig. 17. Unrolling paste bandage on the side of the cake.

Fig. 18. Paste for the side of a square cake.

on either is continuous. At first it might be found easier to make several short strips and piece them together on the cake. Ensure that they do not overlap otherwise a bulge will show on the iced cake.

If possible, leave for several days before applying the first coat of royal icing. This allows the paste to harden slightly, making it easier to work on. However, if time is short, a first coat of icing can be applied immediately, and in fact some people prefer to do so.

Do not replace cake in a tin, but allow to dry out in a cool dry place.

Chapter 3

Royal Icing

What is Royal Icing?

Royal icing is a meringue and is made with egg whites and icing sugar. A little glycerine may be added to prevent it from setting very hard.

As when making meringues, it is essential that all utensils are scrupulously clean and absolutely grease-free. If fresh eggs are used they should be broken and the whites left in a clean, covered container for several hours before use.

Powdered albumen is preferable to fresh egg whites because it is much easier to use and there are no problems of what to do with left-over yolks. For people not connected with the trade it is now possible to buy at least one type of powdered albumen. Large stores and some health food shops stock this and it will be described on the box as a 'meringue mix'. Powdered albumen has, of course, to be reconstituted. Once this has been achieved, the method of making royal icing is the same, whichever form of egg white is used.

HEN ALBUMEN

This is easily obtained by those in the trade, but almost impossible to obtain otherwise. It should be reconstituted by adding 300 ml (½ pint) of cold water to 45 g (1½ oz) of powdered albumen. After stirring well it should be covered and allowed to stand overnight in a refrigerator. Before use it should be strained into a clean mixing bowl. This amount of liquid will take approximately 1·6 kg (3½ lb) of icing sugar.

MERINGUE/ROYAL ICING MIX

This is a fortified albumen. It is available in some large stores and shops, and instructions inside each box explain how to reconstitute the powder. Although I prefer to use hen albumen, I do find that this powder is much easier to use as it dissolves instantly and there is no need to leave overnight before use.

FRESH EGG WHITES

These should never be used straight from the refrigerator. They should be broken into a clean bowl, covered and left at room temperature for several hours. This will cause them to liquefy and make mixing much easier. Great care must be taken to ensure that none of the yolk gets into the egg white. The fat from the yolk will not only discolour the icing but make it impossible to obtain the right texture. Three egg whites will take approximately 450 g (1 lb) of icing sugar.

ICING SUGAR

This should be free from lumps. Always reseal the packet and store in a dry place. Should even the smallest lump be present then the sugar must be sieved before use. The sieve, like all utensils, must be absolutely clean.

GLYCERINE

This may be added to icing made from hen albumen or fresh egg whites. It is stirred into the icing at the end of the mixing and prevents it from setting too hard. I suggest about one teaspoonful of glycerine to every 450 g (1 lb) of icing sugar.

Mixing Icing by Hand

Unlike meringues, the mixture does not require a lot of air beaten into it, as this causes air bubbles to appear in the icing. The action is one of stirring well, rather than beating.

1. Place egg whites into a clean basin and stir in enough icing sugar to give the appearance of unwhipped cream. This will take approximately half the total amount.
2. Add a small quantity of the remaining sugar and stir well for about two minutes. Continue until the desired consistency is reached. For the first coat of icing on the cake it will need to hold its shape when lifted from the basin

on the wooden spoon or spatula (Fig. 19). If the sugar is added too quickly the icing will be dull, gritty and prove difficult to pipe.

3. Scrape down the sides of the basin and cover with a clean damp cloth to prevent the icing from crusting. A plate on top will stop the cloth from drying out too quickly. Royal icing will keep for many days provided the cloth is replaced by a clean one each day. The moisture from the cloth will be absorbed into the icing, however, making it necessary to add more sugar the next time it is used. A plastic basin with an air-tight lid is also suitable for storing icing. There is no need to keep in a refrigerator.

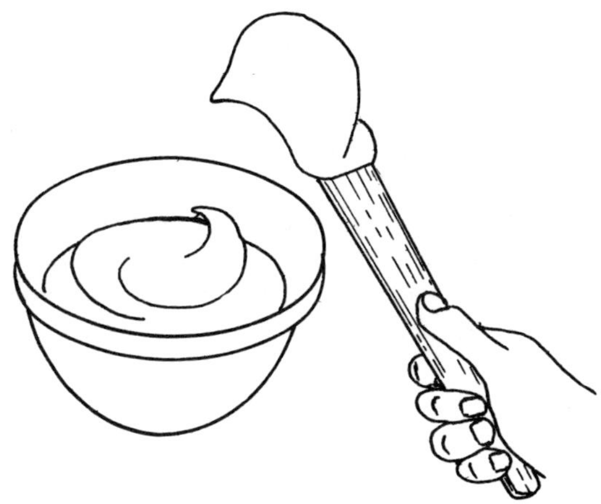

Fig. 19. Spatula and bowl of icing.

Making Icing in an Electric Mixer

Icing can be made in an electric mixer, though I prefer to mix by hand and so avoid the presence of too many air bubbles.

When using a mixer it is essential that it is done at the slowest speed using the beater and not the whisk. Proceed exactly the same as for hand mixing, but beat for only a few moments in between each addition of sugar. The whole operation should not take more than four minutes.

Chapter 4

Coating

This is the most important procedure in icing a cake. A smooth, flat surface is essential as it forms a base to which further decoration can be added.

If the instructions have been followed regarding applying the almond paste or marzipan, the basis is there to produce a well-coated cake. A cake that has been badly pasted can never look good; if the underneath is not right the finished cake will never be so.

Coating the Cake

Prepare the icing as previously described, or if it has been made the previous day, re-stir and add a little more icing sugar if necessary. It is always advisable to have a little extra egg white available so that the icing may be diluted if necessary.

Colour may be added to the icing at this stage if a coloured cake is required. Avoid being too enthusiastic, and use the colouring very sparingly. Aim at light pastel tints, remembering that the colour will darken slightly as it dries.

It is impossible to control the depth of colour if it is poured from the bottle into the icing. A more satisfactory method is to dip the end of a cocktail stick in the colouring and stir this into the icing. Use a clean stick each time to transfer the colour because, if the original one is used repeatedly, hard particles of icing may be transferred into the bottle.

Before starting to coat the cake have the following equipment to hand:

Spatula or wooden spoon.
Turntable.

Palette knives.
Wooden or metal rule.
Side scraper.
Clean damp dish cloth.
Colouring, if required.

ICING THE TOP (Round or square cake)

1. Place the cake board and cake on the turntable and with the larger palette knife put a large quantity of icing on top of the cake. Immediately re-cover the remainder of the icing in the bowl with a damp cloth to prevent crusting (Fig. 20).

2. With the palette knife, spread this icing evenly over the top of the cake and for a few moments paddle down the icing using a backwards and forwards movement. At the same time slowly rotate the turntable with the other hand (Fig. 21). The paddling movement will help to displace any air bubbles that may be in the icing.

Surplus icing will spill down the sides of the cake, and can be removed easily when the top has been coated. Do not forget to wipe the palette knife clean.

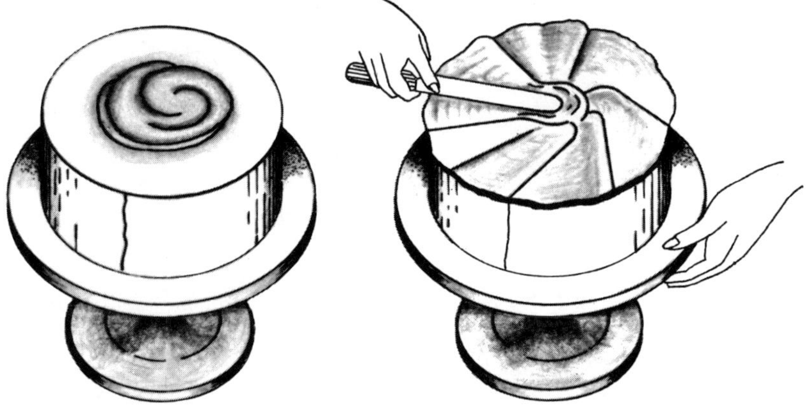

Fig. 20. Placing icing on the top of the cake.

Fig. 21. Paddling down icing on the top of the cake.

3. Holding the wooden or metal rule at the furthest edge of the cake and at an angle of about 45° to the surface, draw it across the cake towards the body, in one continuous movement (Fig. 22). The surplus icing on the rule should be returned to the bowl and the rule wiped clean.

Do not press down too hard with this first coat as the aim is to cover the paste. The subsequent coats will be thinner in order to obtain a fine, smooth finish.

It is difficult, initially, to obtain a satisfactory surface, but a little practice produces remarkable improvement. Should the first attempt not be satisfactory, continue to paddle down the icing and re-scrape the top until a satisfactory coat is obtained. This process can be repeated only for about five minutes, otherwise the icing will start to crust and form hard particles. These cause lines in the coating and give an unsatisfactory finish. If this occurs, leave until the icing is dry and apply another coat.

4. Remove any icing from the side of the cake but, if this feels dry, do not return it to the basin with the rest. It is far better to waste a little icing than to ruin the whole mix (Fig. 23).

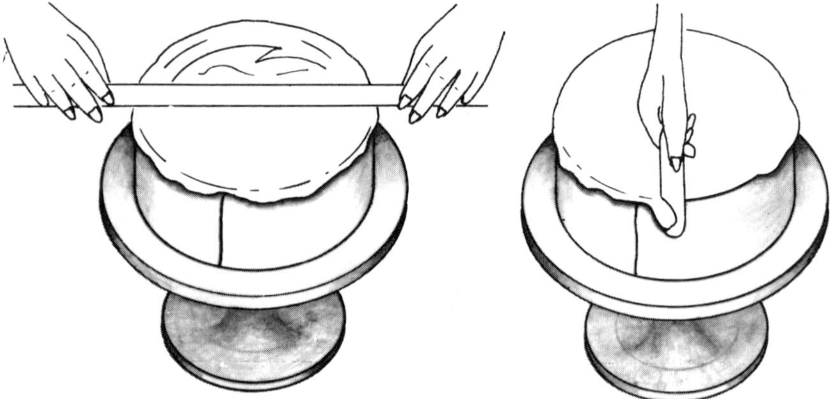

Fig. 22. Rule drawn across the cake.

Fig. 23. Removing surplus icing from the side of the cake.

5. Leave the cake in a dry atmosphere to harden. It is inadvisable to leave iced cakes in a kitchen where they may be in contact with steam. Moisture is absorbed into icing causing it to remain soft.

The top should be dry enough after about two hours to enable icing to be applied to the sides. It is possible to ice the top and sides together, but it is easier to do them one at a time.

ICING THE SIDES (Round cake)

1. Make sure the cake is in the centre of the board and place it on the turntable. Spread icing on the sides with the small palette knife. Paddle it down as on the top of the cake, slowly rotating the turntable at the same time (Fig. 24).

2. Hold the side scraper at a slight angle (approximately 15°) against the side of the cake, and with the other hand take hold of the board at the back of the cake near to the scraper. Slowly revolve the turntable in one continuous movement until a circle has been completed. When the entire surface is smooth, lift the scraper away from the side. This will leave a take-off mark which initially will be very pronounced. With practice and after subsequent coats this mark will be less noticeable.

As when icing the top; several attempts at obtaining a smooth coat can be made before the icing starts to dry (Fig. 25).

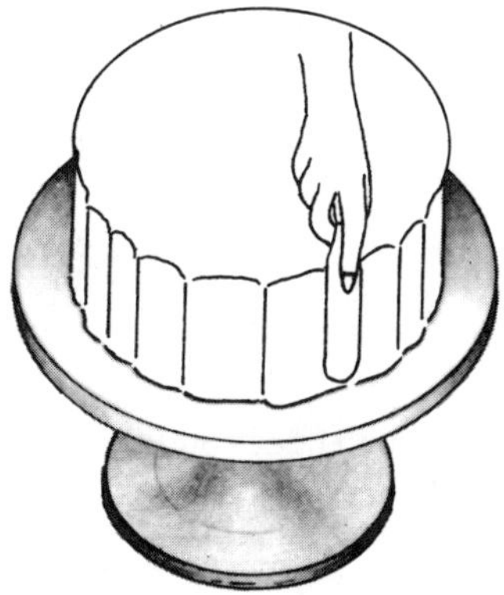

Fig. 24. Paddling down icing on the side of the cake.

Fig. 25. Applying side scraper to the side of a round cake.

Some icing may have found its way on to the top of the cake. As the top coat is dry, it is an easy matter to remove the surplus with a palette knife, leaving the top coat unharmed. Any icing on the cake board should be removed before leaving the cake to dry. Apart from being unsightly, hard icing prevents the smooth movement of the side scraper, resulting in an uneven finish.

ICING THE SIDES (Square cake)

The sides of a square cake are coated and scraped individually. Surplus icing on top of the cake and adhering to the bottom board should be removed before it is dry (Fig. 26).

SUBSEQUENT COATS

One coat of icing is never enough. Two are absolutely necessary and three

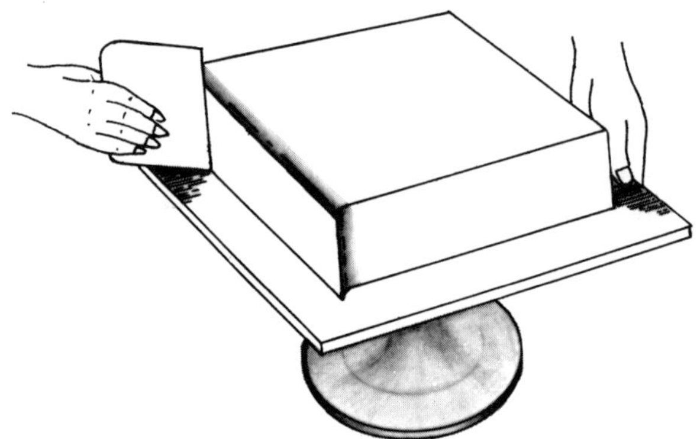

Fig. 26. Applying side scraper to the side of a square cake.

preferable. The beginner may find that it entails four or even five coats before a satisfactory result is obtained.

SECOND COAT OF ICING

When the first coat is completely dry, remove any rough edges and the take-off line with the aid of fine sandpaper. Make sure there are no loose particles of icing on the cake which would spoil the next coat of icing.

Using icing of a slightly softer consistency, apply another coat in exactly the same way as the first. Icing left over from the previous day will probably be the right consistency. It will, however, need to be stirred before use.

THIRD OR FINAL COAT

When the cake has been coated to satisfaction it will require a final coat of icing. This should be softer then the second coat, about the consistency of slightly whipped cream. Icing mixed the previous day is better for this purpose as any air bubbles will have dispersed.

The final coat is applied in exactly the same way as the others, but with a little more pressure applied to the rule and scraper. Most of the mixture is taken off the cake, leaving a thin, smooth film of icing.

Do not use sandpaper after a final coat as this would leave scratch marks on the surface of the cake.

Making a Dummy

Practising coating is very important, but obviously it is not practical to make a cake just for this purpose. If a wooden dummy can be obtained, or made, then this is ideal. An alternative suggestion is to stick together four silver cake boards of the same size with a little icing. These are then stuck on to one board at least 5 cm (2 in) larger. This is coated in the same way as a cake.

To re-use; old icing can be scraped off (or washed off a wooden dummy), sandpapered down, and a new coat applied.

Chapter 5

The Piping Bag

Bags are usually made from good quality greaseproof paper, though some people prefer to use silicone paper. I make two sizes of bag; the larger for shell and rope tubes and the smaller for plain tubes. If in any doubt which bag to use, just remember; the bigger the tube, the bigger the bag. Tubes which only have a small hole only require a small bag.

Greaseproof paper is obtainable in rolls and packets and very often in sheets measuring 38 cm (15 in) by 25 cm (10 in).

CUTTING PAPER FOR A LARGE BAG

Fold a piece of paper 38 cm (15 in) by 25 cm (10 in) diagonally and cut along the fold using a sharp knife. This sheet of paper will make two large bags (Fig. 27).

CUTTING PAPER FOR A SMALL BAG

Fold a piece of paper 38 cm (15 in) by 25 cm (10 in) in half and cut with a sharp knife. This will give two pieces each measuring 25 cm (10 in) by 19 cm ($7\frac{1}{2}$ in). Proceed to fold and cut these papers in exactly the same way as for a large bag. This sheet of paper will make four small bags (Fig. 27).

MAKING A PIPING BAG

The procedure is the same for large or small bags.

1. Hold the paper with the short straight edge between the thumb and fingers of the right hand (Fig. 28(a)).
2. Take the point, in the left hand, and wrap it over and around the right hand (Fig. 28(b)).

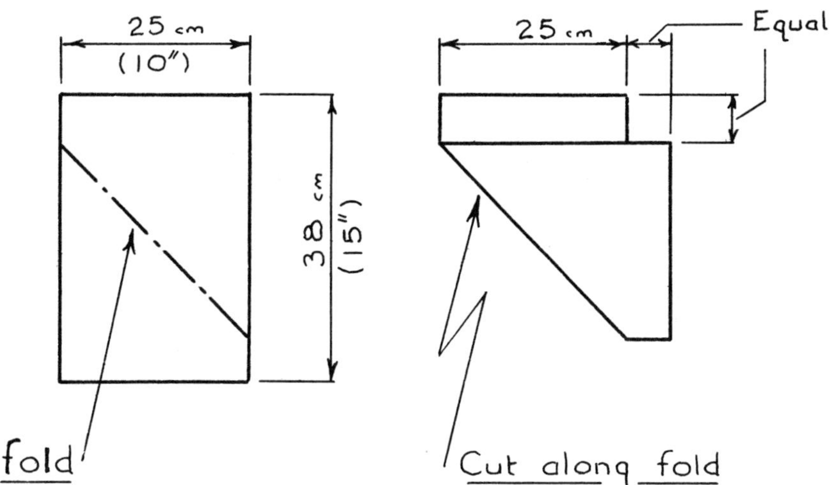

Fig. 27. Cutting paper for bags.

3. Move right hand backwards and forwards, at the same time pulling with the left hand until a sharp point is formed (Fig. 28(c)).
4. Place the left hand on top of the right and take hold of the bag, firmly, with the left hand (Fig. 28(d)).
5. Tuck in flap to make secure. When ready to use; cut 1 cm ($\frac{1}{2}$ in) from bottom of bag with sharp scissors (Fig. 28(e)).
6. Place a tube in the bag and use a small palette knife to transfer the icing. Fold over the top of the bag and roll down neatly, until the icing is reached (Fig. 28(f)).

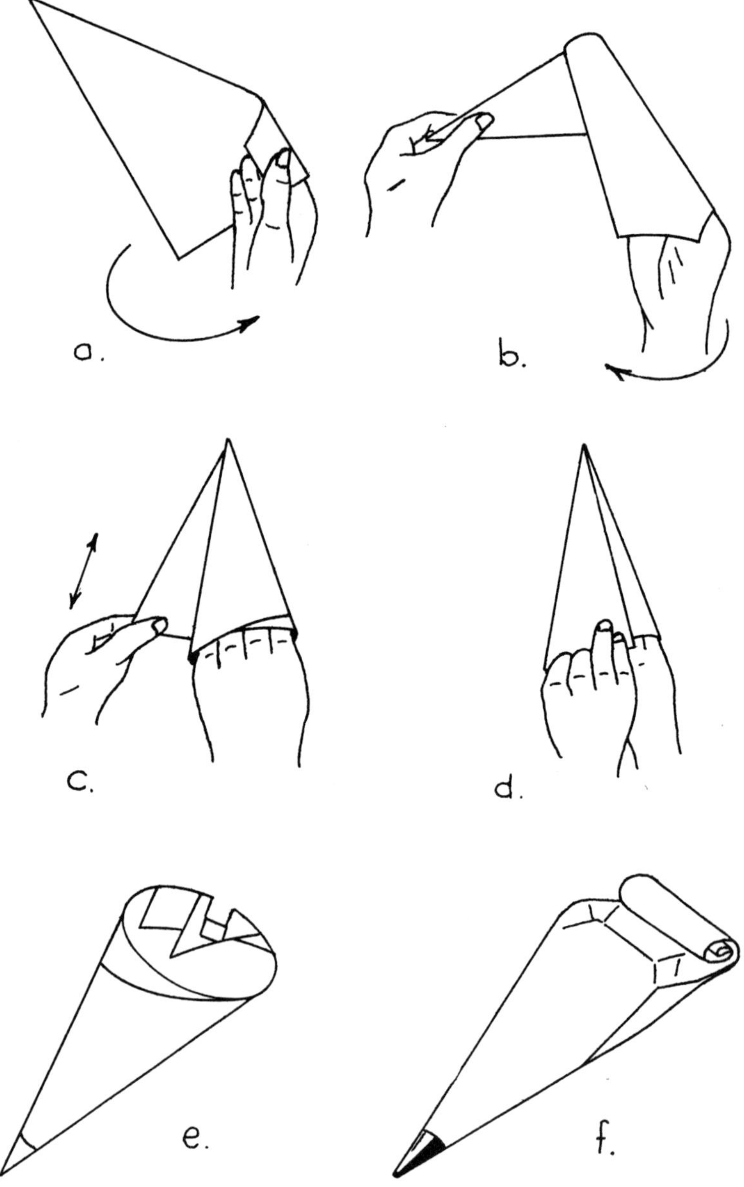

Fig. 28. Bag making.

Chapter 6

Piping Exercises

Before commencing to practise piping, the following equipment should be to hand:

A bowl of royal icing, prepared as for first coating.
Piping tubes (if using the tubes illustrated in Fig. 8, the numbers required are; 0, 1, 2, 3, 13 and 44. These are the only ones used in this book).
Piping bags; large and small.
A practice board (a piece of formica is ideal, especially if it is dark in colour; a chopping board or bread board will also serve the purpose).
A small palette knife.
A damp dish cloth.

Place the tube into the bag (Fig. 28) and two thirds fill with icing, using a small palette knife. Re-cover the icing in the bowl and place the point of the tube into a clean damp cloth. This is to prevent the icing from crusting and causing a blockage in the tube.

The bags are made as previously illustrated, using a small size for tubes numbers 0–3 and the larger size for numbers 13 and 44.

After some practice on a board, border designs should, if possible, be carried out on a dummy. The design should always sit on the top edge of the cake dummy, but not so far over that it would fall off!

There are two ways of holding a bag, the action for linework being different from the pressure needed in executing shell and scroll work. Both ways are illustrated. The following exercises are aimed at covering all the piping which appears in this book.

Straight and Curved Lines

The bag is held in the right hand between the thumb and first two fingers. The left hand assists in holding the bag steady. Figure 29 illustrates this method for piping straight and curved lines where an even pressure is required.

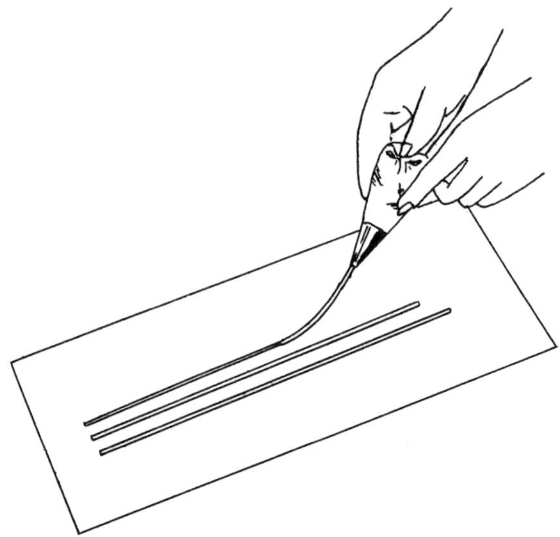

Fig. 29. Holding the bag for piping straight and curved lines.

Do not start pressing the icing out of the bag until contact has been made with the surface.

Touch the surface with the tube, at the same time lightly pressing the bag. As the icing starts to come through the tube, *lift* the tube up from the surface. When the icing is the required length, stop pressing the bag and *place* the icing down on to the surface.

The three words, *touch, lift*, and *place*, are important to remember, since they will assist in achieving the desired results.

If the icing is pressed out of the tube before it has made contact with the surface, or if the tube is not lifted from the surface soon enough, a bulb of icing will be formed. Similarly, if the pressure is still applied after the tube has been placed down, then another bulb of icing will appear on the end of the line.

Even pressure is very important. Too much pressure will give uneven thickness, whilst too little will cause the line to break.

All the exercises in Fig. 30 should be carried out using this method.

Fig. 30(a): These lines should be piped initially with a No. 2 tube. Aim at obtaining straight lines, equal distance apart. After a little practice, repeat the same exercise using a No. 1 tube.

Fig. 30(b): Start this exercise with a No.3 tube. Curves of equal distance are a little more difficult to achieve than straight lines. Place the tube down at the completion of each curve; do not try to complete a line of curves in one movement.

Fig. 30(c): When a line of curves has been carried out satisfactorily (Fig. 30(b)), practise overpiping with a No.2 tube. To make curves more pronounced, overpipe again with a No. 1 tube.

To complete the exercise, continue piping curves parallel to the original line. The object of this is to achieve equal spacing.

Small Scrolls, Filigree and Small Bulbs

SMALL SCROLLS (Fig. 31(a)).
The first three exercises in Fig. 31 are carried out with a No. 3 tube. They are used mainly for overpiping larger scrolls. However they do, by themselves, make attractive and delicate borders piped with either a No. 3 or No. 44 tube.

The bag is held in the same manner as in Fig. 29, but the method of piping is slightly different. After initial contact with the surface, the tube is *lifted only slightly* and touches the surface again just before the scroll is completed. The end of this scroll is drawn away from the surface rather than lifted off. The following scroll should start over the 'tail' end of this scroll to give continuity.

FILIGREE (Fig. 31(b)).
This filigree linework is frequently shown in this book. It is attractive and quite easy to carry out, using a No. 0 tube.

Again the bag is held in the same manner as in Fig. 29, but the tube is in contact with the surface all the time. If the tube is pressed hard against the surface, the icing will not flow through the tube. The action is one of *touching the surface* rather than pressing against it. There is no set pattern to this design and the only important thing to remember is not to cross over any of the lines.

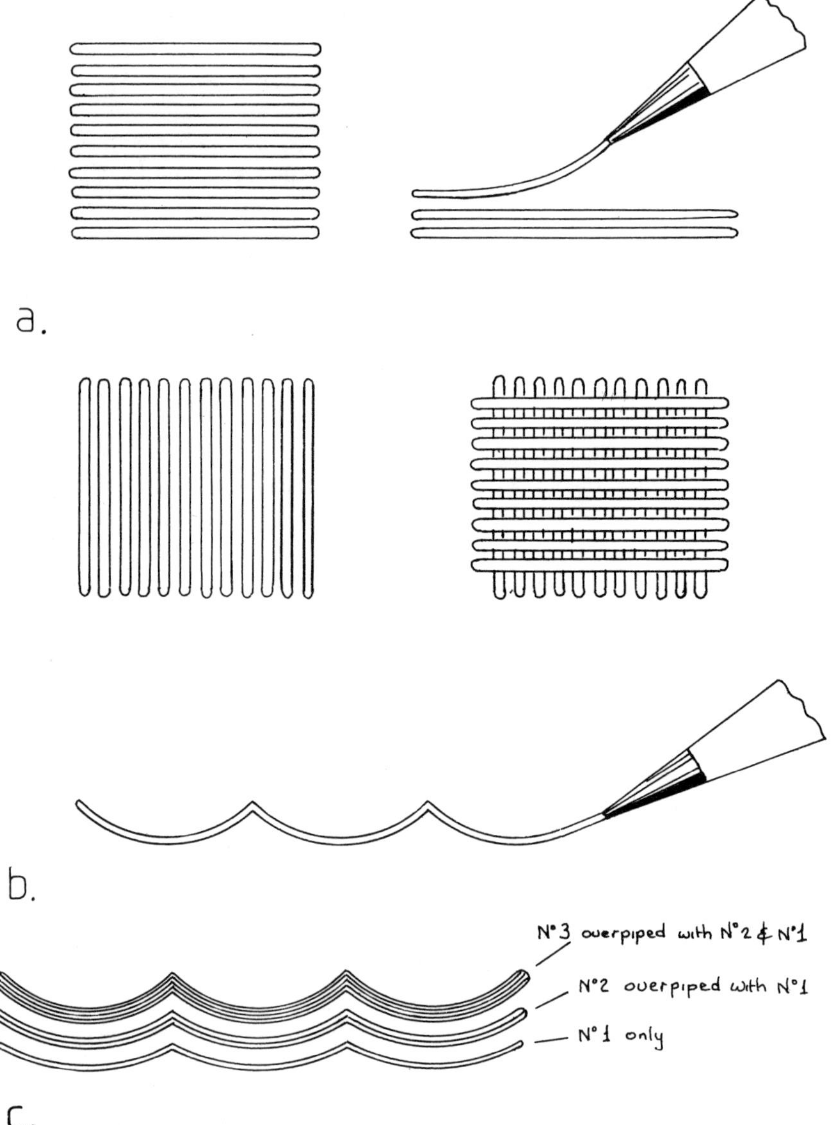

Fig. 30. Piping exercises for straight and curved lines.

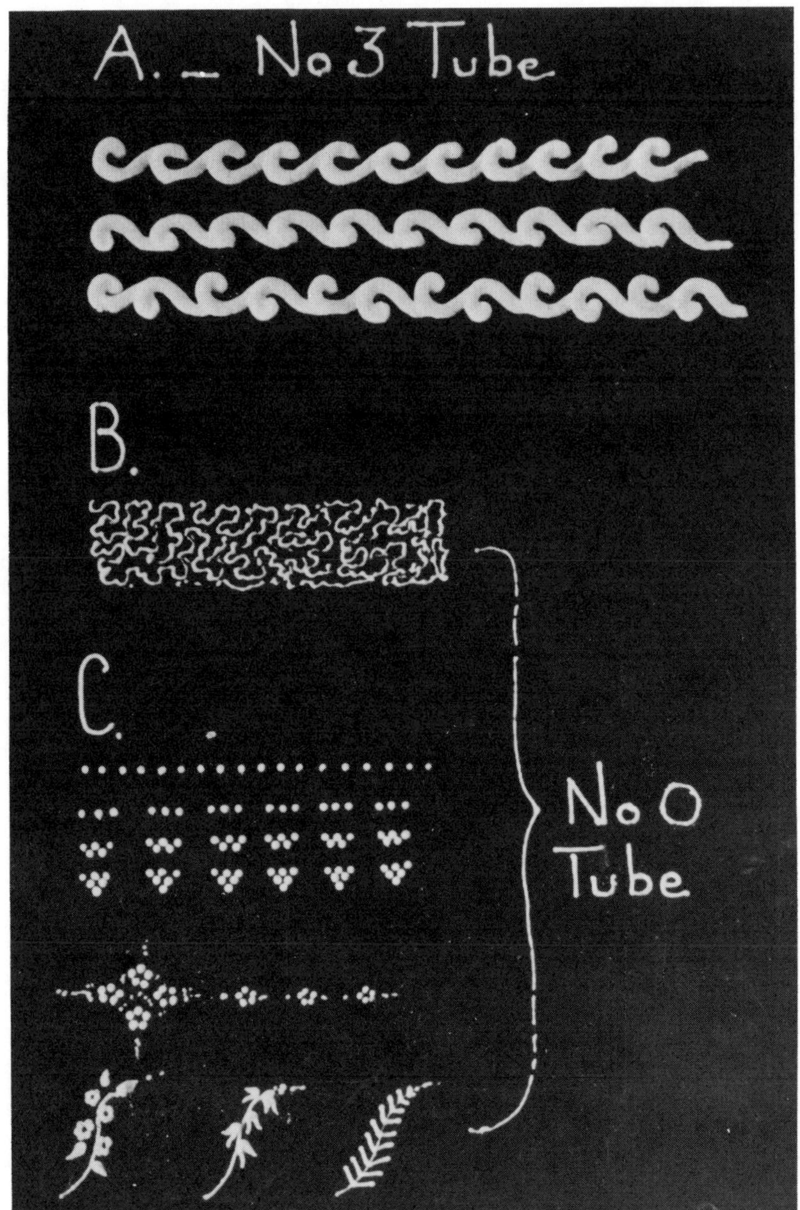

Fig. 31. Piping exercises for small scrolls, filigree and bulbs.

SMALL BULBS (Fig. 31(c)).
Start this exercise with a No. 1 tube and hold the bag in the same way as illustrated in Fig. 29. These small bulbs are used for edging cakes and also to form small flowers and leaves. *Press firmly* against the surface, *stop* and *lift* off. After a little practice using a No. 1 tube, repeat the exercise using a No. 0 tube. By exerting very little pressure and using a No. 0 tube, these bulbs can be made very small indeed. Any 'tails' can be flattened with a fine paint brush.

No. 1 and No. 0 tubes require very little icing in the bag. A small compact bag will allow it to be controlled easily.

Shells, Large Scrolls and Graduated Rope

Because more pressure on the bag is now required, it is held in a different way from the previous exercises. The bag is held in the palm of the right hand and is steadied by the left hand. This enables the icing to be pushed out by the whole hand; rather than just the thumb and two fingers as in previous exercises (Fig. 32).

Fig. 32. Holding the bag for shell and scroll work.

SHELLS (Fig. 33(a)).
The first border piped by the majority of students is a shell. It is much easier to perfect than other types, but still needs quite a lot of practice in order to achieve shells of exactly the same size and shape.

Commercial cakes usually have large shells, but I find that most people prefer smaller ones, which give a more delicate appearance. Whichever is preferred, the action is the same. A No. 13 tube will make a large shell or a fairly small one depending on the amount of pressure put on the bag.

The tube is placed on the surface and the bag kept steady once piping has commenced. The action is to *press firmly* whilst *lifting* the bag *slightly*. When the required size of shell has been formed, stop pressing and *pull* off, making contact with the surface again. If the tube is not taken down to the surface, it will leave a 'tail' on the top of the shell. If carried out correctly, any take-off 'tail' will be on the surface and will be covered by the next shell. You will find, after practice, that the action of making shells becomes one of *push and pull.*

Practise making a row of large shells with firm, even pressure. Using the same tube (No. 13), press lightly to produce a row of smaller shells. Small shells can also be made with a No. 44 tube.

A 'plain' shell can be carried out using a No. 3 tube and this forms an attractive border for the bottom of a cake.

'S' SCROLLS (Fig. 33(b)).

A No. 13 tube is also used to make 'S' and 'C' scrolls. These take longer to perfect than shells and I suggest a guide line be drawn on the board with a No. 1 tube before commencing.

Press the icing out boldly in the same way as for shells, but instead of lifting the tube, gradually release the pressure whilst following the guide line. 'S' scrolls, like shells, should look continuous so always commence the next scroll over the end of the previous one.

A No. 44 tube also produces pleasing scrolls, though they will be smaller than those made with a No. 13 tube. A No. 13 scroll border may be overpiped with a No. 44 tube and again with a No. 3 tube. Often it is finally overpiped with a No. 1 tube.

'C' SCROLLS (Fig. 33(c)).

Carry out in exactly the same way as for an 'S' scroll, following the shape of the guide line. It will be found that a 'C' scroll is completed with a single movement of the wrist, whilst an 'S' scroll requires two.

Overpiping suggested for an 'S' scroll is also suitable for a 'C' scroll border.

GRADUATED ROPE (Fig. 33(d)).

No. 44 is a rope tube, though it has been seen that it can also be used for

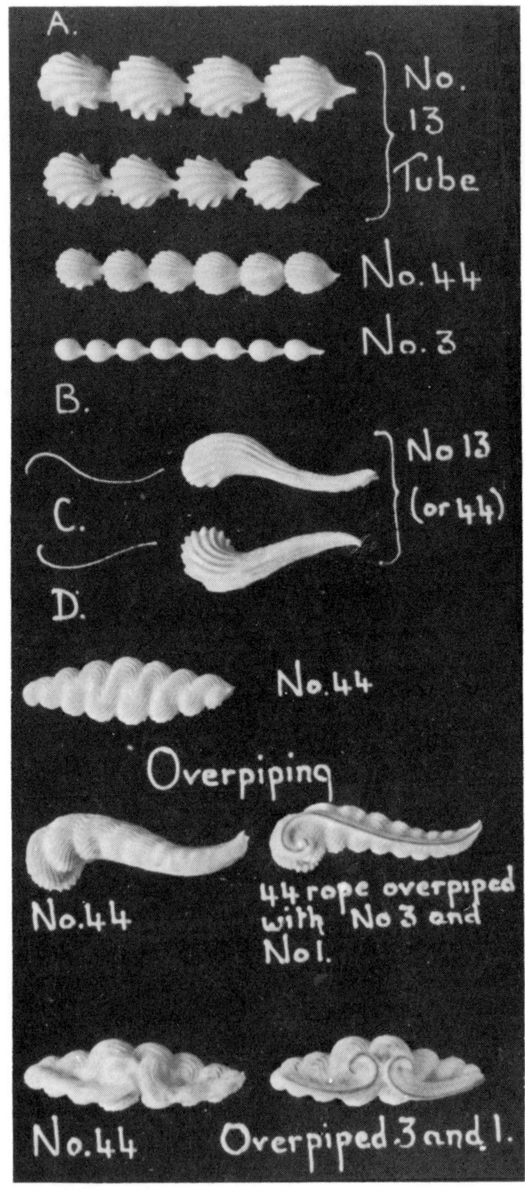

Fig. 33. Piping exercises for shell, 'S' scroll, 'C' scroll and rope.

shells and scrolls. Like scrolls, rope needs much practice and I suggest that small bulbs of icing, equal distance apart, are placed on the board to assist in obtaining regular shapes.

Graduated rope is formed by increasing pressure combined with a spiral action. The side of the tube is placed on the surface and using the wrist, the tube is rotated at the same time as the pressure is increased. When the middle of the rope is reached, pressure is gradually eased and finally the tube placed down on the surface.

Graduated rope is often overpiped with a No. 3 tube followed by a No. 1. As with large scrolls, the tube is not lifted for piping rope, but kept near to the surface all the time.

Chapter 7

Piped Border Designs

After some practice at piping, it should be possible to effect simple borders on a cake.

The illustrations in this chapter are all based on the piping exercises in Chapter 6, and from these basic designs (shell, rope and scrolls) many different borders can be devised. Only a few are illustrated but, by experimenting, many different designs can be created. This is very rewarding and the first step to attaining individuality.

The days of very elaborate borders seem to have passed and now the accent is on simplicity. However, it all depends on the individual choice, and it is better to aim at developing a personal style.

Dividing the Cake for Piping

For a shell border it is not necessary to divide the cake into sections. However, for scrolls and rope it is essential to divide the cake evenly since nothing looks worse than an uneven border. Square cakes present no problems as small bulbs or dots of icing can be placed at regular intervals with the aid of a ruler.

An easy way to divide a round cake is to draw round the bottom of the cake tin with a pencil on to a sheet of greaseproof paper. Cut out this circle and fold into as many divisions as required. Open out the paper and place on top of the cake or dummy. Pipe a small bulb of icing on the outer edge of the cake where the paper has been folded. Re-fold the paper and keep until required again (Fig. 34).

Cakes are usually divided into six, eight or twelve, depending on the size

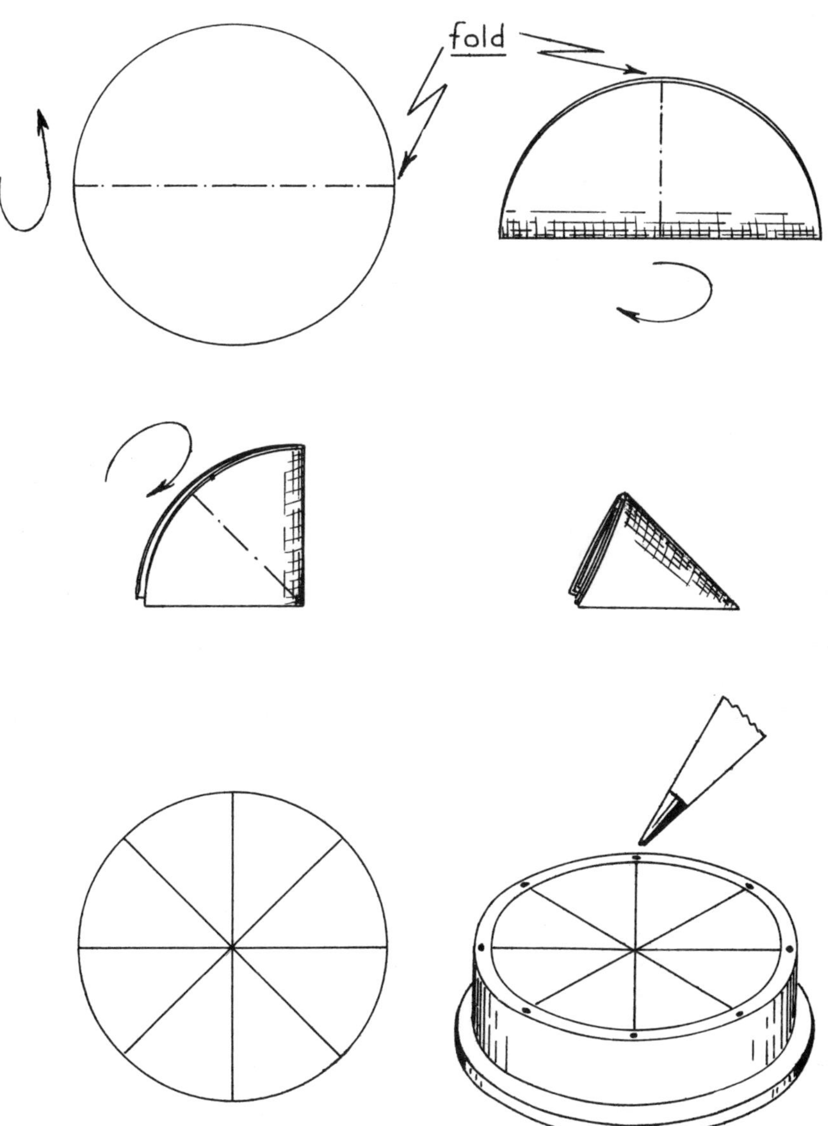

Fig. 34. Template for dividing top of cake.

of the scrolls and also the size of the cake. Large scrolls will look better in large sections and small scrolls will look better in smaller ones.

To divide a cake for a bottom border, place small bulbs or dots of icing on the bottom in line with the bulbs on the top.

At this stage I should mention that the piping on the bottom border must never be smaller than that on the top of the cake. The reason for this is that the cake would appear 'top heavy'. If the piping on the bottom is larger than that on the top, the appearance will be quite satisfactory. This rule does not apply if the bottom board is to be 'flooded out' as the icing then comes almost to the edge of the board.

Never decorate a cake until the surface is absolutely dry, to avoid damaging the coating, and always have the necessary equipment to hand before commencing.

To check that icing for piping is the right consistency, first pipe a little decoration on to a board and if the result is not satisfactory, thicken or dilute the icing accordingly.

Icing required for flooding soft sugar borders has to be thinner than for piping. When icing is being made, some may be placed in a separate bowl before the rest is thickened for piping. Alternatively, it may be diluted afterwards. If possible this icing should always be left for a while to settle and allow the air bubbles to disperse.

It is usual for borders to be the same colour as the cake coating. An exception to this would be a final layer of overpiping carried out in a deeper or contrasting shade.

Border No. 1 – Shell (Fig. 35)

The method of piping shells is explained in the piping exercise in Fig. 33, and there is no need to divide the cake into sections for this border. The shells in Fig. 35 are made with a No. 13 tube, but smaller ones may be made with the same tube using less pressure, or with a No. 44 tube. It is most important that the shells are of equal shape and size. When piping the last shell, a paint brush will assist in placing down any 'tail'. This type of border is relatively easy for the inexperienced decorator and no other embellishment is needed.

Piping on the side of the cake, just underneath the top border, makes a pleasing additional decoration, but only if the piping is first class. These side loops are not as easy to carry out as the shell, and until they can be executed neatly it is advisable to be content with a plain shell border. The side piping is explained in the following instructions for border No. 2.

Fig. 35. Shell border.

The bottom border is piped in a similar way as the top border making sure that the shells always touch the side of the cake.

Border No. 2 – Combined 'S' and 'C' Scrolls (Fig. 36)

This delicate top border is carried out using a No. 3 tube. It is executed in the same way as the piping exercise in Fig. 31(a), and the linework on the side as the piping exercise in Fig. 30(c).

The piping on the side of the cake does take some time to perfect. Place the tube (No. 3) on the top edge of the cake making sure that the icing has adhered to the surface before applying pressure to the bag and lifting the tube. Experience is required to judge the correct amount of icing to be pressed out to ensure that an even loop is obtained each time the tube is placed down again. When the line of loops has been piped around the cake with a No. 3 tube, they are overpiped with a No. 2 tube and an additional line of loops piped underneath with the same tube. Both lines are then overpiped using a No. 1 tube and a single line of loops using the same tube piped underneath.

The top border may be used with or without the side piping. The bottom border shown in Fig. 36 is another shell, but smaller, using a No. 44 tube. As the top border is very delicate a heavy border on the bottom would not be suitable and would give an unbalanced appearance.

Fig. 36. Combined 'S' and 'C' scroll border.

Border No. 3 – Double 'S' Scrolls (Fig. 37)

For this border the cake must be divided into sections. Start by etching guide lines in each section with a No. 1 tube. This is shown in the illustration and the section on the right demonstrates the commencement of the piping.

With a No. 44 tube pipe a scroll using a roping action described in the piping exercise in Fig. 33. Instead of increasing the pressure and then decreasing it again as when piping graduated rope, the pressure is applied at the beginning to form the head of the scroll and then gradually decreased. A second smaller scroll is piped in such a way as to sit on the outer edge of the cake. By the time the last scroll has been piped, the first one should have crusted enough to enable overpiping to commence.

Still using a No. 44 tube, follow the line of the scroll and pipe a plain 'S' scroll over the top. This is the only time when linework is carried out differently from that previously explained. Instead of lifting the tube and then placing the line of icing down, the line is piped touching the scroll underneath. This does not produce a good line as the icing settles into the grooves of the scroll. However, it does produce a good base for the next layer of overpiping.

The next layer is piped with a No. 3 tube directly over the top of the No. 44. This is carried out by the usual touch, lift and place method.

Finally, the linework is overpiped with a No. 1 tube, usually in a contrasting colour or a deeper shade of the colour being used, although this is not essential.

Linework is also performed inside the scrolls. Start with a No. 3 tube and follow the shape of each scroll using the touch, lift and place method. Overpipe this line with a No. 2 tube and place another line of No. 2 alongside it. Both lines may be overpiped with No. 1 if desired.

The bottom border may be carried out in the same way as the top, but as this is rather ornate, a simple shell or flooded border (see Fig. 44) may be preferred.

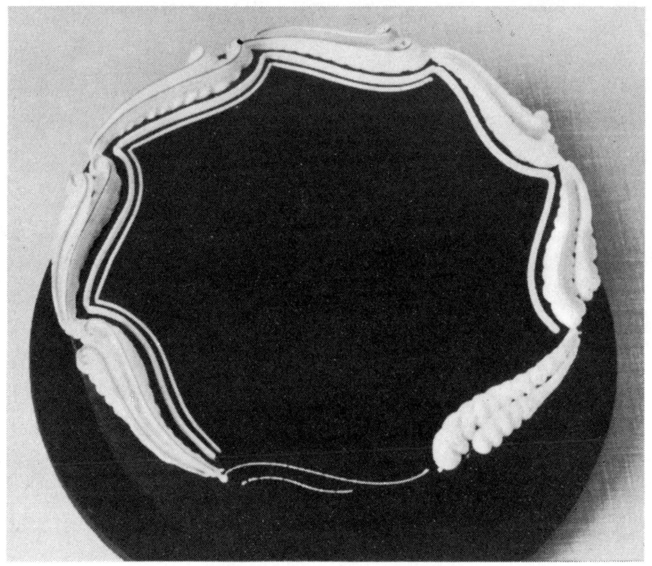

Fig. 37. Double 'S' scroll border.

Border No. 4 – Graduated Rope (Fig. 38)

This border, like the previous ones, is suitable for round or square cakes and the cake must be divided into equal parts.

With a No. 44 tube pipe graduated rope in each section as in the piping exercise in Fig. 33. Still using the No. 44 tube, pipe two 'C' scrolls on to each rope as illustrated in the overpiping in Fig. 33. As with the first layer of overpiping in the previous border, this line is overpiped into the rope instead of being placed down on to it. This ensures that the icing settles into the grooves and that the next layer of overpiping, when done in the usual way, is smooth and even.

Overpipe the No. 44 'C' scrolls with a No. 3 tube, using the touch, lift and place method, and finally overpipe with a No. 1.

Linework inside the border and on the top outside edge is carried out with tubes Nos. 3, 2 and 1.

The bottom border may be done in the same way as the top or a flooded border, as shown, may be preferred (see Figs. 43 and 44).

Fig. 38. Graduated rope border.

Border No. 5 – Soft Sugar (Round) (Figs. 39, 40 and 41)

Many different designs may be made by folding and cutting a piece of greaseproof paper the same size as the top of the cake (Fig. 39). This piece of paper is placed on to the top of the coated cake and the outline marked

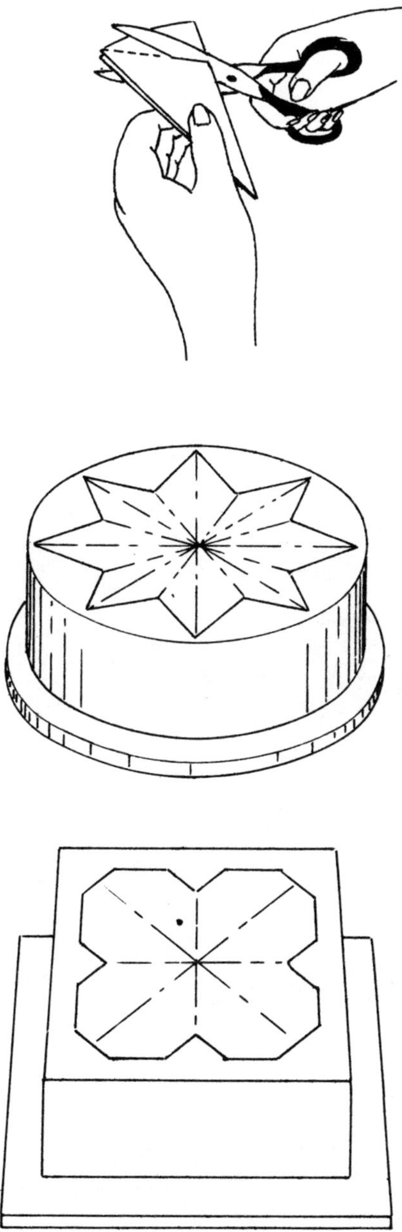

Fig. 39. Templates for flooded top borders.

with a series of dots or lines using a No. 2 or No. 1 tube. The paper is then re-folded and put away for future use.

Follow the linework using a No. 3 tube. Do not pipe directly over the marks, but about 4 mm ($\frac{1}{8}$ in) outside them. These marks will be covered by the icing when the design has been flooded. It is essential to ensure that each line joins, or the icing will flow through.

Pipe a shell border round the outside of the cake with either a No. 13 or No. 44 tube, but keep the shells quite small. A slightly larger shell border may be piped for the bottom border.

Dilute some icing with egg white or albumen and place in two large bags, taking care not to fill each bag more than half full. Always use two bags even if one would be sufficient. If one bag should break, another bag of icing is immediately available.

When diluting icing, stir in the egg white or albumen gently until the correct consistency is reached. Beating will cause air bubbles which spoil the

Fig. 40. Flooding the top border (round cake).

finished appearance. The icing should resemble thick cream and should not leave the mark of the spatula when lifted from the bowl. If it is too soft, however, it will flow over the linework when flooding the cake. Very little practice is required before the correct consistency is achieved.

Cut the end of one bag and proceed to flood between the No. 3 outline and the shell border. Flood generously using a paint brush to disperse any air bubbles, and to assist in taking the icing into corners and obtaining a smooth finish.

Do not flood the complete border in one continuous movement but flood a small section of the border about 5 cm (2 in) wide. Before it has been allowed to crust, continue flooding similar sections on alternate sides of the first one, i.e. first the left-hand side and then the right-hand side. By progressing around the cake in this manner the icing will remain reasonably fluid and no join will be visible where the final sections meet.

The flooded sections are made more attractive by covering with filigree linework using a No. 0 tube (piping exercise in Fig. 31). It is essential that the icing has thoroughly dried before the filigree is piped. Consequently it is preferable to leave the cake overnight to dry, or at least for several hours.

Linework using tubes Nos. 3, 2 and 1 may be placed inside the flooded border.

Fig. 41. Brushing out the flooded top border.

Border No. 6 – Soft Sugar Border and Flooded Board (Figs. 42, 43 and 44)

Folding a piece of paper the same size as the top of the cake, cut a template and proceed in the same way as for the previous top border. Once the flooding of the top border has been completed, (Fig. 42) place a No. 1 tube in a small bag and half fill with icing of piping consistency.

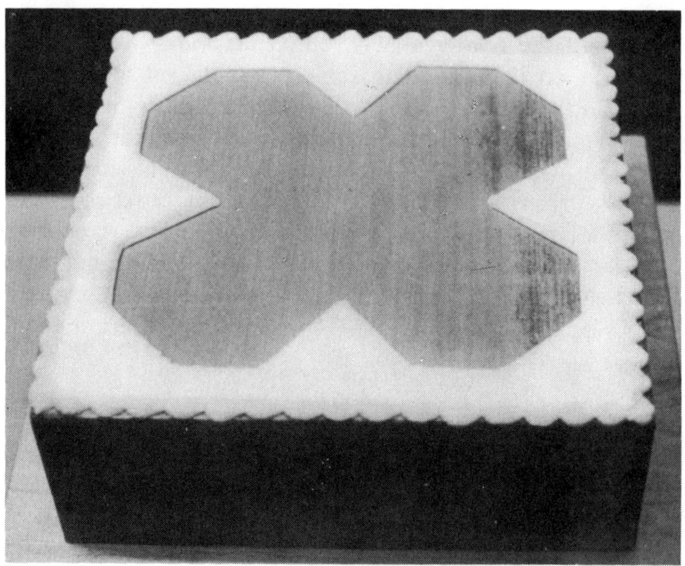

Fig. 42. Flooding the top border (square cake).

Using the No. 1 tube, pipe a straight line 1 cm ($\frac{1}{4}$ – $\frac{1}{2}$ in) inside the edge of the board. Try to complete a whole side without a break in the linework and make sure that there are no gaps in the icing where the linework is joined at the corners. This linework is done using the touch, lift and place method, and it will be seen that to get a really straight line, the tube has to be lifted, though not pulled, well away from the board. If breaks do occur in the icing, make sure that the joins meet otherwise the softened icing will flow through.

The procedure for a round cake is the same except that it may be done in one continuous movement instead of four for a square cake.

When doing this border on a round cake, the piping is done with one hand whilst the other hand slowly revolves the turntable allowing a continuous

Fig. 43. Outline for a flooded bottom border.

Fig. 44. Flooding the bottom border.

line to be piped. It might be found easier at first to pipe these outlines with a No. 2 tube instead of a No. 1 (Fig. 43).

The flooding for the bottom border is carried out in the same way as for the top. Apply a liberal amount of icing between the cake and the outline and brush smooth. Do not flood more than 8 cm (3 in) at a time to avoid the edges drying out (Fig. 44). As with the top border, filigree is piped on top of the flooding after the icing is dry.

The border is completed with a series of dots (see the piping exercise in Fig. 31, Chapter 6) using a No. 0 tube, and a similar edging may be piped inside the top border or it may be finished with linework as previously described.

Flooded bottom borders look good with any type of piped border and particularly with the runout top borders which will be described in a later chapter.

Chapter 8

Lettering, Inscriptions and Monograms

Many people are of the opinion that a cake is imcomplete unless it includes an inscription. I disagree and believe that unless it is essential or has been specially requested, then it should be dispensed with. A cake with holly and bells does not require the word 'Christmas' to be added. If the decoration signifies the occasion (and it should) then no further explanation is required.

This does not mean that inscriptions and numerals should never be used, and in fact there are occasions when they are necessary. For instance, a personal monogram on a cake is very desirable, but only if the lettering is first class and instantly readable. Numerals look attractive only if they form part of the design.

I believe the question should be, 'Is it necessary?'. If the answer is 'Yes', then it must be carried out skilfully. All too often a well piped cake is completely spoiled by a badly piped inscription. It is often thought that lettering is easy to learn and quick to carry out, but this is far from the truth.

Even simple runouts are regarded as 'advanced work' by most schools, although I find that new students are quite able to cope with them. However, lettering, which appears at the beginning of most courses should, in my opinion, be regarded as 'advanced work'.

Lettering

Good lettering not only requires a lot of practice, but also a lot of thought. The size of lettering has to be considered in relation to the size of cake, and the overall space that it will take up has to be worked out in advance. Then there is the style of lettering to be decided upon and finally the spacing, which all too often seems to be forgotten.

There are many types of lettering suitable for royal icing and this is another instance where developing your own style is so important.

PIPING DIRECTLY ON TO THE CAKE

The most popular alphabet and the one most suitable for practice is Roman. Start by using a No. 2 tube and, when the whole alphabet has been satisfactorily completed, change to a No. 1 tube and repeat the exercise.

Lettering is piped in a similar manner to straight and curved lines (Fig. 30), i.e. touch, lift and place. The amount of icing lifted from the tube will depend on the size of the stroke being piped. Capital letters will require the tube to be lifted away from the surface more than small ones (Fig. 45).

ABCDEFGHIJKLMN
OPQRSTUVWXYZ
abcdefghijklmnopq
rstuvwxyz

Fig. 45. Roman alphabet.

It will be necessary to practise on a board or dummy many times before piping directly on to a cake. When piping on a cake, use a No. 2 tube with icing in the same colour as the cake coating. Overpipe this with a No. 1 tube using a contrasting colour.

Here are some important points to remember:

1. Never change the style of lettering when piping an inscription. The only exception to this would be the capital letter.

2. Always pipe the inscription on to a board or write it down on paper before piping it directly on to the cake. This way you will find out how much space it will occupy.

3. If the inscription is meant to be in the middle of the cake, then make sure it is. To help obtain this, place a small mark in the centre of the cake and start by piping the middle letter of the inscription over the mark. If the

inscription has an even number of letters then the mark would come in between the middle two letters. As some letters occupy more space than others (the letter L obviously takes less space than the letter W) this method is not entirely accurate, but acts as a good guide (Figs. 46 and 47).

Fig. 46. Lettering in the centre of a round cake.

Fig. 47. Lettering in the centre of a Square cake.

4. If the inscription is not to occupy a central position on the cake, then it must be balanced by a suitable motif (Fig. 48).

5. Concentrate on making the spacing of the letters look right. Some letters will require a larger space between them than others. The aim is not to leave an even gap between each, but to achieve a well balanced word.

6. Lettering looks best horizontal and I never advocate the use of vertical lettering. A piece of cardboard or a short ruler placed gently on the cake will act as a guide for piping a straight line.

7. For piping on a curve it is essential that a template be made in order to achieve accuracy. This can be made with greaseproof paper, but if cut out of cardboard it can be kept and used many times (Fig. 49).

Several inscriptions for lettering suitable for piping directly on to a cake are shown in Fig. 50.

RUNOUT LETTERING

It has been seen that lettering can be piped directly on to the cake, and an alternative way is to use a different type which is suitable to be filled in with softened icing.

This method can also be carried out directly on to the cake by outlining

Fig. 48. Creating balance with lettering.

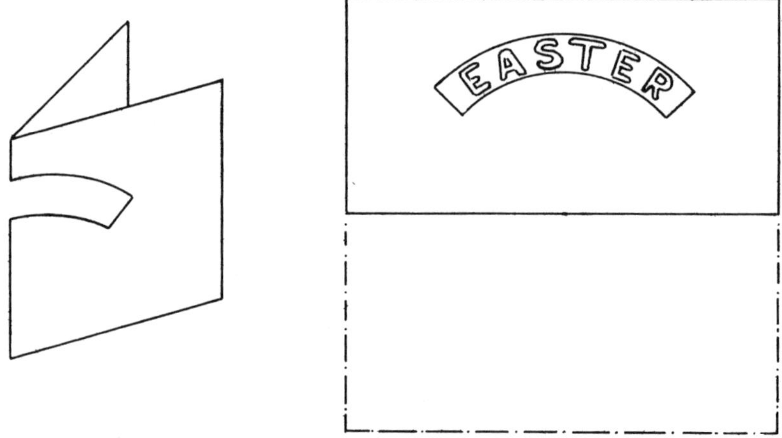

Fig. 49. Template for lettering on a curve.

Fig. 50. Lettering suitable for piping directly on to a cake.

the letter with a No. 1 tube. Slightly softened icing is then placed into a small bag and a hole, no larger than a No. 2 tube, is cut from the end. The outline is then filled in with icing, using a fine paint brush to take the icing into the corners.

As with all runout work, a little practice is required to obtain the right consistency. If the icing is too soft it will flow over the outline. If it is too stiff, it will be impossible to achieve a smooth surface.

At this point I would say that I prefer this form of lettering to be carried out on waxed paper and transferred to the cake when the lettering is dry. This is known as 'runout' work and is the best and easiest way of achieving good lettering.

The method of achieving runout lettering is as follows:

1. Draw or trace the required letters on to greaseproof paper.
2. Place this paper on to a piece of board or glass and stick down each corner with a little icing.
3. Place a piece of waxed paper, shiny side up, on top of the drawing and stick this down also.
4. Outline the letters with a No. 1 tube, using the same colour of icing as will be used for the filling.
5. Half fill a small bag with softened icing and, having cut a small hole from the end, fill in the letters with the aid of a fine paint brush.
6. Leave to dry under a lamp or about 62 cm (2 ft) from a warm electric fire for about ten minutes. This will give a gloss finish to them when dry.
7. Leave overnight in a dry place; preferably a drying cabinet or an airing cupboard.
8. To assemble; peel gently off the paper and place them on the cake. When satisfied that the positioning is correct, stick on to the cake with the use of a little icing in a No. 1 tube.

Some types of lettering enable each letter to be flooded in one movement. However others will require some strokes to be done separately in order to achieve an easily recognisable letter (Fig. 51).

Fig. 51. Runout lettering.

As runout lettering takes up more space than the piped type it is often used only for capital letters, whilst the rest of the inscription is piped. However, whether the inscription is done entirely in runout lettering or a combination of runout and piping, largely depends upon the size of the cake and any other decoration to be used.

It is also possible to runout part of a letter and pipe the rest. The letter N in the word 'NOEL' in Fig. 47 illustrates this.

Numerals are also best carried out by this runout method. Both take very little icing and can be made days or weeks in advance and stored in a box until required. Figure 52 shows numerals suitable for being runout. An important point regarding runouts which must be emphasised is that the icing must not contain glycerine. This would cause the runouts to remain soft.

Fig. 53 shows some types of lettering that are suitable both for outlining and flooding directly on to the cake, runout on to waxed paper, or a combination of runout lettering and direct piping.

Monograms

Monograms look very good in royal icing. They are particularly pleasing on wedding cakes, where the bride and groom's initials can be depicted producing something unique.

They are always piped on to waxed paper before being placed on to the cake. They need to be carefully designed and drawn and it is essential that the drawing is placed under the waxed paper to enable an accurate reproduction to be piped.

I believe that monograms look better in ornate lettering rather than block and I have compiled an alphabet for this purpose (Fig. 54). The letters for a monogram have to be combined in such a way that they look right together. They must not run along side each other and should cross in at least one place. In order to achieve balance it is possible to make one letter larger than the other. Some letters just do not fit together and I have added a few extra letters which might help in composing monograms. These are only a guide; they may be altered, made larger or smaller and, if necessary, the strokes of some made longer or shorter.

Monograms are executed in exactly the same way as single runout letters. The drawing is placed under waxed paper and is then outlined with a No. 1 tube before being filled in with softened icing. The one difference is that monograms are never completed immediately, but always done in sections.

Two or more colours may be used but one colour must always have been

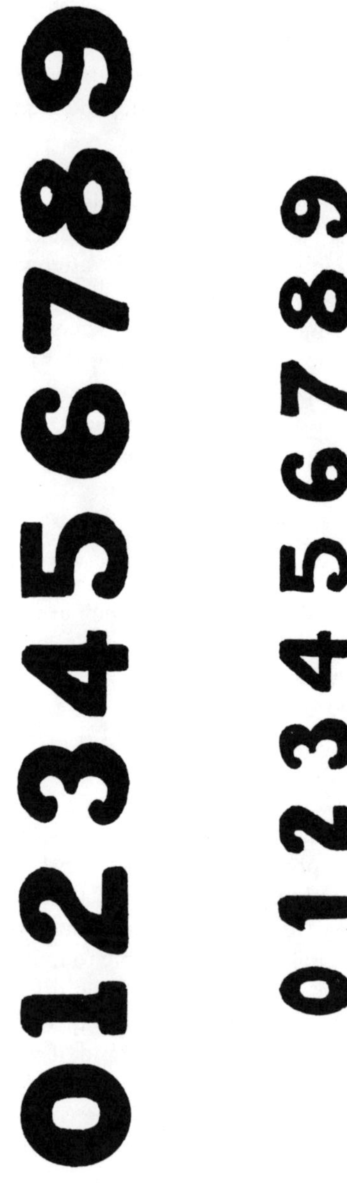

Fig. 52. Runout numerals.

John PAUL

MICHAEL

DORIS

ELAINE

Kathryn

Fig. 53. Runout capitals and inscriptions.

ABCD
EFGH
HIJK
LMM

Fig. 54. Runout alphabet.

N O P Q

R S T

U V W

X Y Z

Fig. 54. – Contd.

Fig. 55. Monograms.

left to dry for a few minutes before a different one is put next to it, otherwise one colour would run into another.

After some practice, it might be possible to dispense with the outline and flood softened icing straight on to the drawing through a small hole cut in the bag. However, I never advocate this for the beginner as it is much less frustrating to outline insubstantial runouts than to risk them merging.

Monograms may be decorated when dry with small flowers or linework. More decoration may be added after they have been assembled on the cake. It is not possible to show a combination of every letter, but I have illustrated a few in Fig. 55. Combining monograms is fascinating and many different designs may be made using the same two or three letters.

Though occasionally used to decorate the top of cake, they are usually placed on the side. This means that the depth of the cake must always be kept in mind when designing the letters.

Lettering dried flat will fit the side of any square cake, but in order for them to fit a round cake they must be kept quite small. If larger letters are required for a round cake then the monogram must be dried on a curve similar to that of the side of the cake.

Chapter 9

Runout Figures

Runout work is the most interesting aspect of royal icing and also the most rewarding. Provided that simple motifs are chosen initially, no problems should be encountered. In fact, not only do I find that students take delight in being able to create something edible, but they experience no difficulty in carrying it out. I have never understood why this form of decorating is considered by so many to be beyond the scope of the beginner.

The method of producing runout figures is similar to the runout lettering described in the previous chapter. You must first decide what form of decoration the cake should have, and this should include the side of the cake and the border design. Never start to decorate a cake until the finished product, including the colour, has been determined. This is true of every cake whatever form of decorating is required. This does not mean that it is necessary to draw the cake, but to have in mind what the final result should be.

Some people think that they cannot pipe figures unless they can draw them. This is not so and the only skill required is the ability to trace. Ideas can be acquired from many sources, the most popular one being greetings cards. After a while it will be found impossible to pass such stands without searching for further ideas for runouts! Other ideas come from gift wrapping paper, children's books and dress materials. Of course, it is ideal if one is able to design and draw, but it is not essential.

Although I have already covered border designs, in practice the cake top is always decorated before the border is piped. This avoids the border being damaged whilst working on the top of the cake.

In this book I include many drawings which may be traced and used for producing runouts.

Here are some important points to note before commencing:

1. Waxed paper is required for all runouts. It must be free from creases and thin enough for the drawing to be seen through it.
2. The board or piece of glass, on which the runouts are piped, must be absolutely straight otherwise they will not dry flat.
3. Softened icing is required for this work and it must be diluted with egg white or albumen. Water would weaken the solution and the runouts would not dry. It must not contain glycerine.
4. Runouts must be prepared in a dry atmosphere. Steam from a kettle or a washing machine will be absorbed into icing and this is another cause of runouts remaining soft.
5. A lamp or small electric fire is necessary to direct heat on to the runout and assist with the initial drying. This will ensure the runout dries with a pleasing gloss.
6. When completed, runouts must be left to dry out thoroughly. This takes anything from a few hours to two days depending upon the size of the runout and the drying temperature. Most people do not have a drying cabinet which is specially designed for this purpose, but an airing cupboard will also do quite well. It is important to remember that they must be left in a dry and preferably warm place. Moisture of any kind will cause colours to run and the runouts to remain soft.
7. Runouts are ready when they can be peeled away from the waxed paper.
8. Features, etc. are painted on the runout with a fine paint brush using edible colouring. They must be absolutely dry before this can be done.
9. Small figures take very little icing and small bags are always used. Even if only one motif is required, it is as simple and almost as quick to make two. One might get broken, but if not, the other can be stored in a box and used at some future date.
10. A separate drawing is required for each runout. It is inadvisable to remove a drawing from underneath a wet runout.

There are some runouts which require to be outlined with a No. 1 tube before being flooded in with softened icing, though for the majority this can be dispensed with. As a rough guide, I would say that if the figure is very thin (as was seen to be the case with lettering) then the runout should be outlined first. The same colour must be used for the outline as for the flooding.

Candle and Bell

A candle and a bell are shown in Figs. 56 and 57. Both are very simple and will present no problem for the beginner. There is very little difference between these and the more complicated runouts; if these can be achieved, so can others. The only difference will be that some are made up of many small sections and require several different colours.

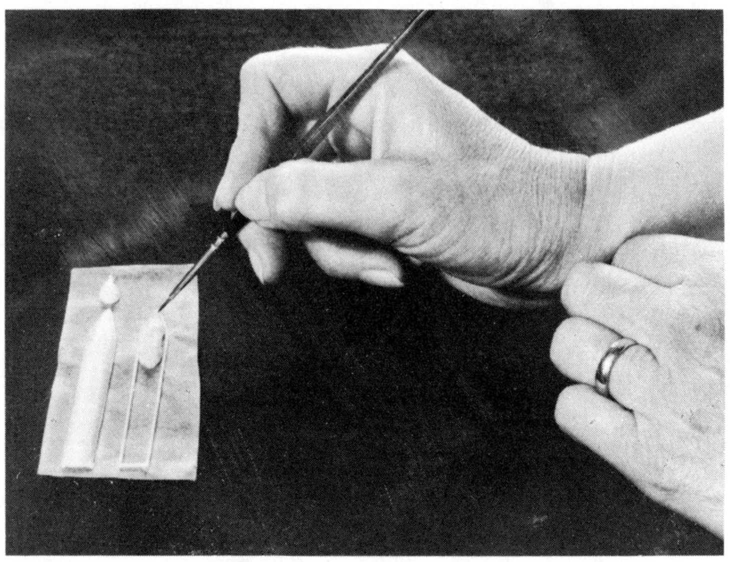

Fig. 56. Flooding a candle.

Suppose that to decorate a cake we require one red candle and two white bells. To ensure against breakages two candles and four bells have been drawn, and the procedure is as follows:

1. After checking that all necessary equipment is to hand, place the drawings on to a flat board and stick down with a little icing.
2. Place a piece of waxed paper, shiny side up, on top of the drawings and stick this down also.
3. Using icing of piping consistency, colour a small amount bright red and place in a small bag with a No. 1 tube. Only mix a very small amount on a saucer using a cocktail stick to transfer the colouring to the icing. Make sure the colour is thoroughly blended with the aid of a small palette knife.

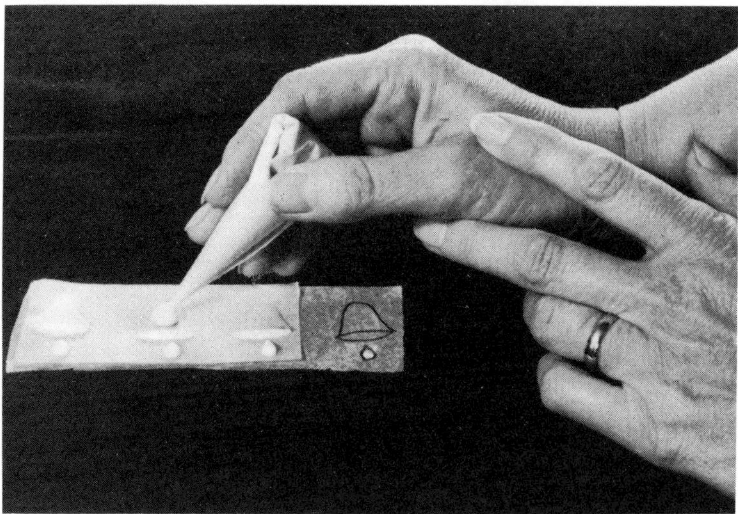

Fig. 57. Flooding a bell.

4. Dilute the remaining icing to a soft but not runny consistency. The aim is for the icing to be able to be brushed smooth, but not too soft that it will flow.
5. Half fill a small bag with white icing. Colour a little of the remaining icing yellow for the flame and place in another small bag. A third bag is required for bright red icing of the same tint as the red outline.
6. Wash cloth, saucers and palette knife and place the ends of the bags and the No. 1 tube in a damp cloth.
7. Using the touch, lift and place method, outline the candles with the No. 1 tube. Cut a small hole from the bag of yellow icing not larger than a No. 2 tube and press out on to the flame. Brush to the outer edges with the aid of a fine paint brush.
8. After cutting a similar hole from the end of the bag of red icing, squeeze out the icing into the outlined candle. Do not be afraid to press out the icing boldly. It will not overflow the outline unless the consistency is too soft. Too little icing will produce a flat candle. Use the brush to obtain a smooth, even surface (Fig. 56).
9. Cut the end from the bag of white icing and flood in the bottom (underside) of the bells. Although the whole of the bell will be white, it cannot be completed in one movement otherwise the icing would run and the shape would be unrecognisable.

10. The clappers can be flooded on to the waxed paper, though some might prefer to pipe these straight on to the cake with a No. 2 tube. As these are so small, very little pressure is required when flooding the outline.
11. Leave under a lamp for a few minutes for the icing to crust over, before flooding the rest of the bells. Make sure that this part of the bell is really thick so as to contrast, with the underneath (Fig. 57).
12. Leave to dry as before for about ten minutes before putting in a dry place.
13. Always be sure to keep the board flat until the runouts are absolutely dry.
14. When dry, the yellow flames are painted with a few streaks of orange or red colouring to make them more realistic.
15. When completely dry, runouts can be stored in single layers in boxes until required.

To Place Runouts on the Cake

Runouts are peeled gently off the waxed paper and placed on to the cake. When sure that the position is correct, they are stuck with a little icing. The coating must be absolutely dry before the runouts are assembled otherwise the moisture would dissolve the runouts. If a wick is required between the candle and the flame it is piped directly on to the cake with a No. 1 tube using brown icing.

Both the bell and candle that we have just dealt with are very versatile. Although the candle is mainly used for Christmas cakes, it can be used as a simple decoration for a child's birthday cake, using pastel colours. The bell is ideal for wedding and anniversary cakes when carried out in the same colour as the cake coating, and can be placed on either the top or sides. A pale lemon Easter cake looks very good with pale lemon bells. For decorating the top of Christmas cakes the bells need to be in bright colours and more decoration may be added with a paint brush after the runouts are dry and before they are placed on to the cake. If they are being used for the side of a Christmas cake, they may be carried out in the same colour as the cake coating. They will still signify the occasion and yet not detract from a more colourful decoration on the top.

For painting runouts a very fine, preferably sable, paint brush is required. Edible paste colours are better than liquid colours for this purpose as they are more concentrated.

Never use colour straight from the bottle or jar. Place a small amount in a saucer and, in the case of paste colours, apply a *little* water if necessary.

For a simple Christmas decoration, the candle can be used alone. Holly leaves make an attractive additional decoration and yet are easy to accomplish. The holly leaf is runout on to waxed paper and does not require to be outlined, although the inexperienced decorator may prefer to do so. I have provided a drawing for a holly leaf, though I feel this should not be necessary as leaves of irregular shapes and sizes look more realistic when put together. Veins are painted with green colouring after the runouts are dry.

Fern is piped directly on to the cake with a No. 0 tube in either green or brown. For the stem, the tube should lightly touch the cake. This may cause a few gaps to appear in the line, but gives a more realistic appearance than when using the touch, lift and place method. The spikes are piped using the touch, lift and place method, but as these are very short it will be found that the tube is only lifted slightly.

Figure 58 shows the simple runouts that we have covered, used for Christmas decoration. The fern has been piped after the candle has been assembled and before the holly leaves have been arranged. The design can

Fig. 58. Candle and bell assembled on a dummy.

be modified easily by using the candle without the leaves and fern, or two candles instead of one. In fact, many variations could be devised from this simple design.

The piped border is one that has been covered in Chapter 7.

Curved Runouts (Marguerite)

Most runouts are dried flat, but there are exceptions, and one of these is the marguerite. This flower is quite simple to do and makes a very attractive decoration. It needs to occupy a central position on the cake and is an ideal centre-piece for wedding, anniversary and birthday cakes.

On a tiered cake, it can be used for the centre of the lower tiers whilst a taller decoration in the form of a vase of flowers is placed on top. However, it is not essential for a wedding cake to have a tall ornament and I like this flower on the top tier of a wedding cake. It not only presents 'something different', but assists in achieving total edibility.

The marguerite is simple to draw, but for those not wishing to do so, I have provided an example in Fig. 59.

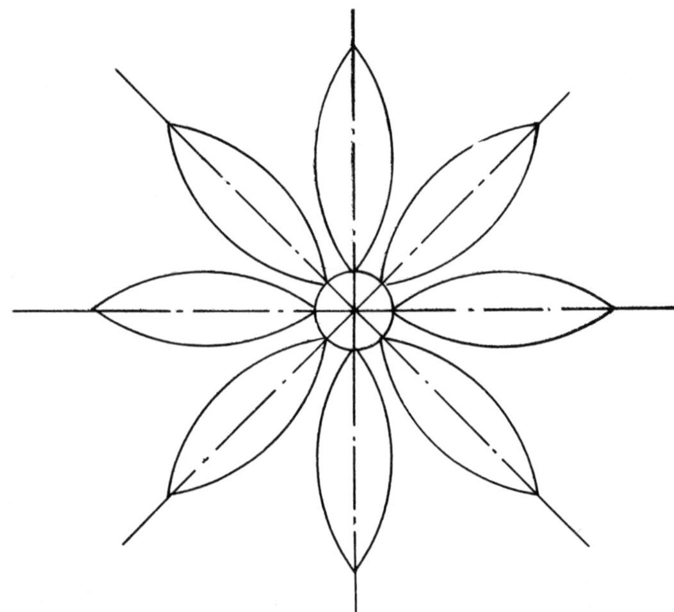

Fig. 59. Drawing of a marguerite.

Once the flower has been drawn, only *one* tracing is used regardless of the number of petals required. This is in direct contrast to the flat runouts where a separate drawing is required for each one. The reason for this is that the petal is piped flat on to the waxed paper as previously described for the candle and the bell, but is lifted immediately from the drawing and placed into a suitable curved dish to dry. The disc for the centre of the marguerite is dried flat. As with all runouts, extra ones must be made to allow for breakages. This marguerite requires eight petals and therefore I suggest that twelve be made, plus two discs for the centre.

Here are step by step instructions for piping a marguerite. In addition to the usual equipment, a fruit or cereal dish is required.

1. Place the drawing of a petal on to a board and stick the corners down with icing. (One petal and the centre disc may be traced from Fig. 59.)
2. Cut twelve pieces of waxed paper, not much larger than the drawing, and place one of these over the drawing, making secure with a little icing. The waxed paper used for petals should be as fine as possible to enable it to bend easily when placed on a curved surface.
3. Outline with a No. 1 tube and immediately fill in with softened icing. Do not overfill, using icing as stiff as possible for runout purposes. This prevents the icing from moving to the bottom of the petal when placed in the dish and causing the shape to be distorted.
4. Place the petal into the dish immediately, and secure with two small bulbs of icing from the No. 1 tube.
5. When sufficient petals have been completed, flood two discs (outlining first if wished) and leave to dry with the petals. Dry under a gentle heat for about ten minutes and then place in a warm dry atmosphere until thoroughly dry (Fig. 60).

To Assemble the Marguerite

The marguerite is assembled directly on to the cake as follows:

1. Find the centre of the cake and make a small mark in the coating with the point of a knife (cut a piece of greaseproof paper the same size as the cake top and fold into four pieces).
2. With a No. 2 or No. 3 tube, pipe a bulb of icing over the mark and place the disc on top. Do not press the disc right down but leave a small gap between the disc and the cake in which to place the petals.
3. Gently peel a petal from the waxed paper and place one end into the icing

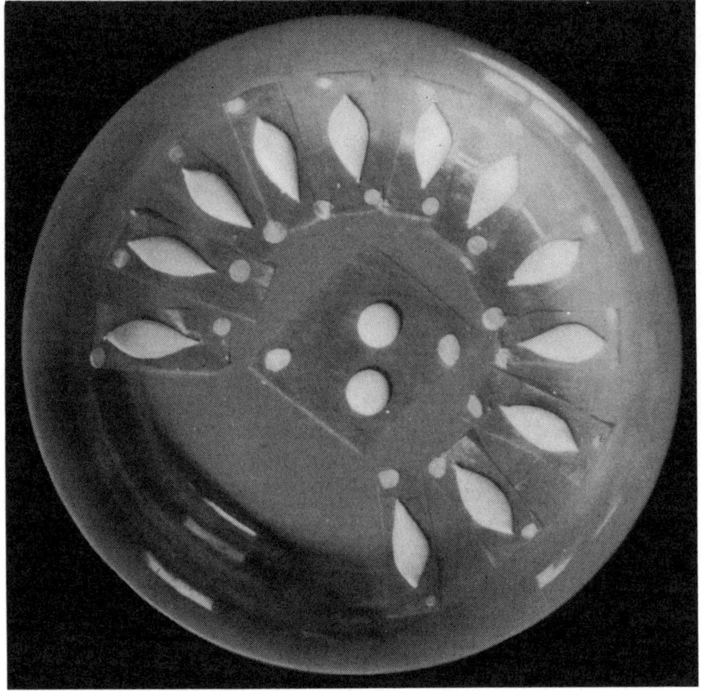

Fig. 60. Marguerite petals in a dish.

under the disc. It may be necessary to place a wisp of cotton wool or a small block of plastic foam under the petal to keep it in an upright position until set.

4. The next petal should be placed opposite the first and the remainder equally spaced until eight have been assembled.
5. When the petals are secure, the cotton wool or foam, if used, should be removed. Stamens are piped on to the disc when the petals have completely set. They are piped with a No. 0 tube with icing slightly stiffer than normally used for piping, in whatever colour is desired. Hold the tube vertical over the disc and press out the icing as for a small bulb. Lift the tube away whilst still pressing the icing out and so produce a point. Pipe as many as desired.

Figure 61 shows the marguerite and a border which has already been described in Chapter 7. It will be seen that although the same bells are used for the side of the wedding and the Christmas cakes, they are quite suitable for both.

Fig. 61. Marguerite assembled on a dummy.

Raised Runouts (Butterfly)

I have shown that most runouts are dried flat and placed on to a flat surface when completed. A few, such as the marguerite, are dried on a curve. Another type, also dried flat, are the ones raised when assembled on to the cake. Typical of this is the butterfly.

The butterfly, like the bell, is very versatile and can be used on wedding, anniversary and birthday cakes. A great many different drawings can be made in a number of sizes around the basic shape. It is suitable for use on the top and sides of a cake, simply by varying the size.

Whatever design is used, the procedure is the same; the wings and body are piped separately on a flat surface. The butterfly wings in the figure have been outlined since they are of delicate design, but there is no need to outline the body which is completed in three sections (Fig. 62).

This butterfly contains filigree linework, but it need not be included. By flooding the entire wing an attractive butterfly can be produced, and the method of assembling it is exactly the same. The equipment required for this runout is the same as previously described.

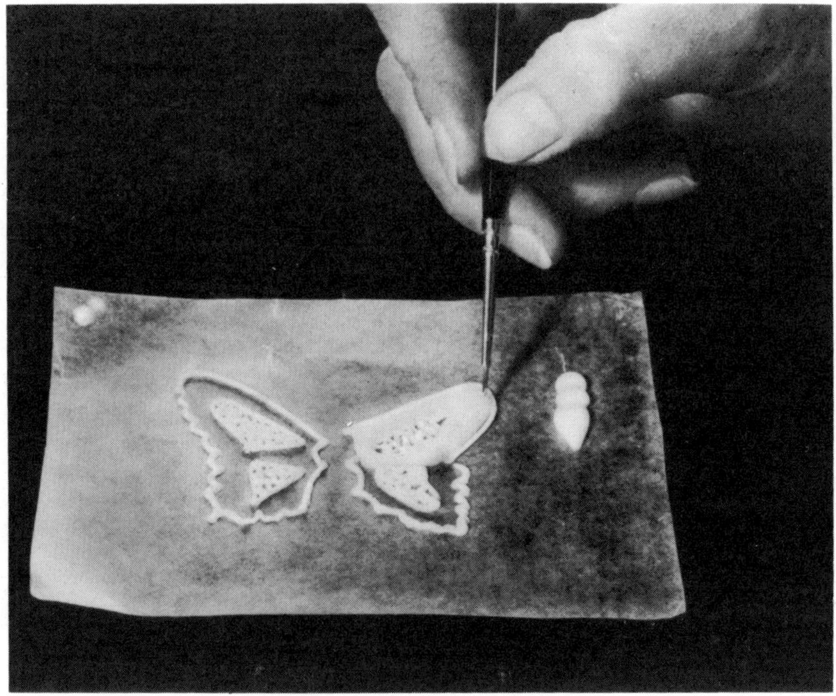

Fig. 62. Flooding a butterfly.

1. Place waxed paper, shiny side up, over the drawings and outline the wings with a No. 1 tube.
2. Using a No. 0 tube, pipe the filigree linework ensuring that the lines touch without crossing, especially on the outer edge. If the linework does not make contact with the outline, it will not hold together when the butterfly is peeled from the waxed paper.
3. With softened icing, flood between the outline and fill the middle portion of the body.
4. Leave to dry for about five minutes before filling in the top and bottom portions of the body.

To assemble, the body is placed on to the cake and stuck down with a little icing from a No. 1 tube. A little icing is piped on to the wing where it is placed against the body and it is held in place with a wisp of cotton wool or foam (Fig. 63). The same procedure is followed for the other wing. The cotton wool is removed after about fifteen minutes when the icing has set. The antennae are piped on to the surface with a No. 0 tube. Very small but-

Fig. 63. Butterfly assembled on a dummy.

terflies are often used to decorate the sides of cakes and because they are so light they will not require any support. It is normally sufficient to place a small amount of icing from a No. 1 tube on each wing and hold them against the cake for a few moments.

Chapter 10

Runout Plaques

Another simple runout, which has many uses, is the plaque. Numerous shapes and sizes can be made in various colours. They can be made weeks or even months in advance, and they are suitable for decorating the top or sides of cakes.

The plaque is made in the same way as other runouts and is dried flat. It is always outlined with a No. 1 tube, using icing of the same colour as used for the flooding.

There is one important difference from the runouts previously described. The softened icing must have been made several hours previously and left to stand, covered, to disperse any excess air bubbles. This is not absolutely necessary with small runouts but with plaques and runout collars it is essential. Bubbles which appear on a plain surface look unsightly and spoil the finished appearance.

As previously mentioned, the icing for runout purposes must not contain glycerine. It will need to be stirred gently before being placed in the bags.

After the shape has been outlined on to waxed paper, it is flooded and made smooth with the aid of a paint brush. The brush is also used to prick any air bubbles which might appear. As most plaques contain quite a lot of icing, a large bag is required. Do not fill the bag more than half full and always have an extra bag of icing available to ensure that the plaque can be completed without having to stop to fill more.

When flooded, put under a gentle heat for several minutes to encourage a gloss finish. Leave in a warm atmosphere for several days and then store, still attached to the waxed paper, until required.

The outlines of the plaques in Figs.64–67 may be traced straight from the book. Plain plaques can be decorated in numerous ways. Here are a few examples of the sort of decoration that may be used.

Fig. 64. Runout plaques.

Fig. 65. Runout plaques.

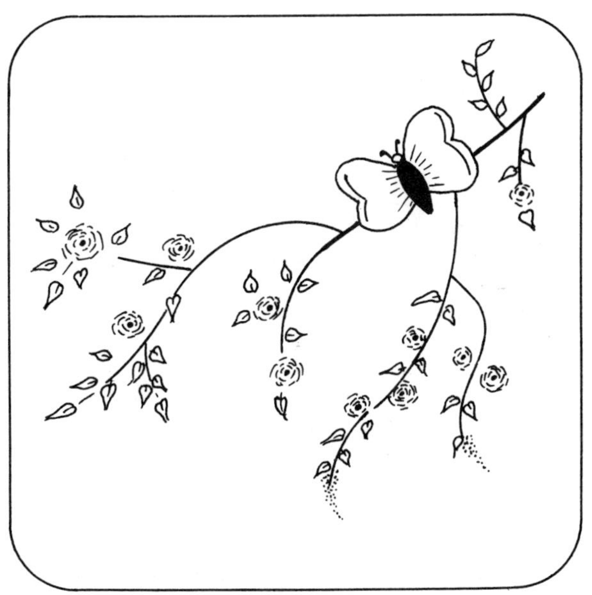

Fig. 66. Runout plaques.

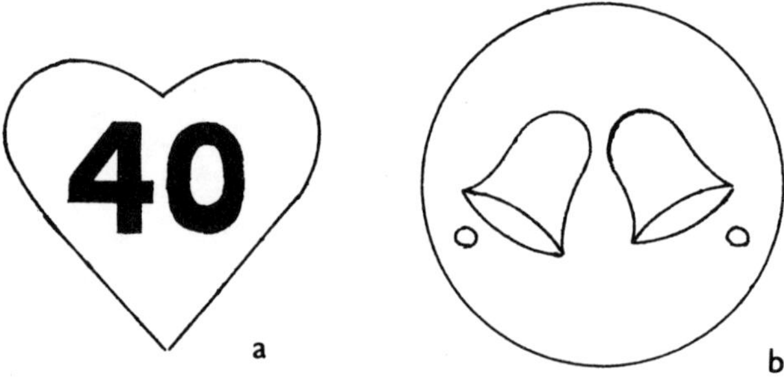

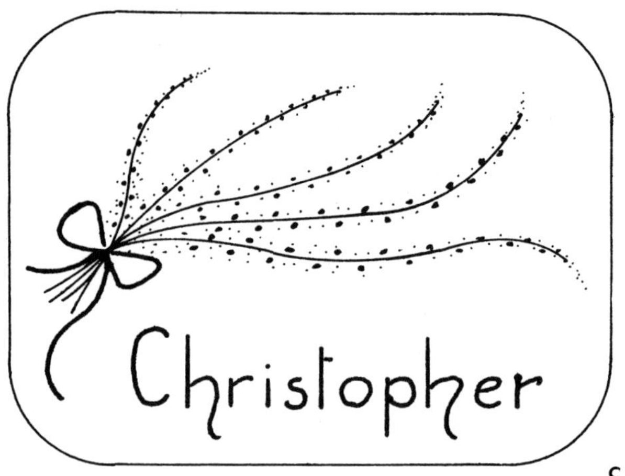

Fig. 67. Runout plaques.

1. Painted with Edible Colours

A design is painted directly on to the plaque. It is usual to draw or trace the design first on to tracing paper or greaseproof paper. The paper is then turned over and the drawing outlined again on the reverse side. Turning the paper yet again, it is placed on to the plaque and the outline traced for the last time with a sharp pencil using as little pressure as possible. Too much pressure might cause the plaque to break. When the paper is removed, the design should be clearly visible and ready to be painted with a fine paint brush.

Figure 64(a) is an example of a painted plaque. It is a small plaque suitable for the sides of a cake for someone who plays badminton.

2. Design Piped Directly on to the Plaque

This may be in the form of a simple spray of flowers, probably combined with a name. Piping on plaques should always be as delicate as possible and therefore executed with a tube no larger than a No. 1.

Figure 67(c) provides an example of piping on to a plaque. The spray of heather is piped with a No. 0 tube. The stem is piped first in brown with the tube gently touching the plaque. Tiny bulbs of purple are then piped against the stem with even smaller dots of green. The bow is also piped with a No. 0 tube and the lettering with a No. 1 tube overpiped with a No. 0. A design such as this would not need to be traced on to the plaque.

3. Combination of Painting and Piping

This is usually a painted motif combined with a piped inscription. Fig. 65(b) is one such example. The wrought iron work is painted brown, the small holly leaves green and small spots red, to represent the berries. The middle section of the lantern is painted orange and allowed to dry before the remainder is painted brown.

The design does not need to be traced except, perhaps, the lantern. If an inscription is desired, it could be piped with a No. 1 tube in the colour of the plaque and overpiped with No. 0 in brown.

4. Runout Motifs, Lettering and Numerals

Small runouts are suitable for mounting on to plaques. They may be used with or without lettering or numerals for such occasions as twenty-first or silver wedding cakes. Assembled runouts such as the marguerite can be put together on a small plaque, and monograms for the side of the cake can be similarly treated. Inexperienced decorators sometimes feel happier to place delicate runouts on to small plaques rather than risk breaking them when actually placing them on the cake.

Figures 64(b), 66(a), 67(a) and 67(b) all illustrate the points just made.

Figure 66(a) is a plaque for the top of a twenty-first birthday cake. It also has runout shamrocks. Figures 64(b), 67(a) and 67(b) are suitable for the sides of a cake.

5. Combination of Painting and Runouts

It is quite possible to paint a scene and also include a runout. The runout must be of a delicate nature. Figure 66(b) illustrates a painted plaque which also has a small runout butterfly. The butterfly wings were dried flat and placed at an angle when assembled on the plaque. The design was not traced.

6. 'Special' Plaques

Often a cake is required for a particular school or society and the design can incorporate plaques reproducing their badge or emblem. These can be painted or reproduced in royal icing. Two examples are shown in Figs. 64(c) and 65(a).

Figure 64(c) is the badge of St. David's College, Llandudno. The background colour is dark turquoise and because the correct shade was available in a paste colour, the plaque was outlined and flooded in turquoise. Had only liquid colour been available, the plaque would have been made white and painted afterwards. Deep colours are difficult to achieve with liquid colouring and often the amount of colouring required reduces the icing to a point where it will not set hard.

In order to obtain a 'raised' effect the lion was runout, in white, in twelve separate pieces. These were painted gold when dry, and stuck on to the plaque using the original tracing as a guide for assembling. An alternative way would have been to trace the design on to a white plaque and paint it gold before painting the background turquoise.

The plaque Fig. 65(a) is the emblem of the Donkey Breed Society. The outline of the plaque could have been made larger to decorate the top of the cake, but I felt it was more suitable to be used as a side decoration.

The plaques were outlined as previously described and flooded with white icing and left to dry. The donkey's head and also the initials were then traced on to the plaques. These were then painted with a fine paint brush using edible brown colouring. When the linework was completely dry, the background was carefully painted in royal blue, using liquid colouring. If it is found that one coat of colour does not give the required depth, it is better to apply another coat after the first has dried, thus avoiding making the plaque too wet and so causing the icing to dissolve.

Here are a few general points regarding iced plaques:

1. The outline is always piped using the touch, lift and place method.
2. If the plaque is to be on top of the cake it is usual to place it in a central position. It is peeled gently from the waxed paper and a little icing placed on the back before it is stuck on to the cake.
3. It adds to the decoration if an edging is piped around the plaque with a No. 0 tube, and this is always done after the plaque has been stuck on to the cake. The only time it is not suitable is when the plaque is a reproduction or an heraldic design and therefore only the original decoration should be copied. Small dots or bulbs shown in the piping exercise in Fig. 31 are suitable for the edging.
4. Gold and a silver colourings are not easily available but can be obtained from a few companies, some of which have a mail order service. It should be emphasised though, that although non-poisonous, they are not permitted food colourings and should be used for decorating purposes only.

Chapter 11

Ribbons, Bows and Edible Corner Pieces

Ribbons and Bows

Ribbons and bows play an important part in cake decorating. Although they are artificial decorations, they can be easily removed from the cake without impairing the appearance. They form a decoration that is soft and delicate to the eye, and do not transmit the brashness and commercial look of plastic.

When choosing ribbon for decorating cakes, three things should be considered.

1. The width of the ribbon: Very narrow ribbon around the side of a deep cake looks out of place, but it should not be so wide that only very little of the icing is visible. If the cake is between 6 and 8 cm ($2\frac{1}{2}$ and 3 in) deep then the ribbon should be between 3 and 4 cm (1 and $1\frac{1}{2}$ in) wide.

2. The material: The most suitable ribbon for cakes is satin. However, this is now quite difficult to acquire and is being replaced by nylon ribbon.

3. The colour: This is very important; an inappropriate ribbon can completely spoil a well-iced cake. The occasion as well as the colour of the cake are to be considered when selecting the colour of the ribbon. Pale-coloured cakes are enhanced with a ribbon of the same or slightly deeper shade of the cake icing. If this is not possible, a contrasting colour should be used. White cakes require white ribbon unless another colour has been introduced into the decoration and this colour can be used for the ribbon.

A looped ribbon and a sewn bow are illustrated, both are suitable for round or square cakes.

LOOPED RIBBON

These attractive ribbons are made from a piece of ribbon about 30 cm (12 in) long. A small bag is also required with icing of piping consistency and the same colour as the ribbon. Cut a small hole from the end of the bag; it is then ready to use for sticking the loops together.

Take the ribbon in the left hand, and with the right side of the ribbon facing, turn back approximately 5 cm (2 in) and hold between the thumb and finger (Fig. 68(a)).

Still holding the ribbon in the left hand, take hold of the rest of the ribbon in the right hand and lift it to make another loop about 1 cm ($\frac{1}{2}$ in) below the first. Hold this between the thumb and finger of the left hand whilst making a third loop in the same way (Fig. 68(b)).

Separate the loops with the fingers and pick up the bag of icing with the right hand (Fig. 68(c)).

Place a bulb of icing between each loop and gently press together, care being taken not to crease the ribbon (Fig. 68(d)).

Put the ribbon down and leave to set whilst making the remainder of the ribbons. A small mark may show through the ribbon where the last bulb of icing was piped, but this is less pronounced if icing of a similar colour to the ribbon is used.

If the ribbon is plain, small flowers may be piped with a No. 0 tube. This gives additional decoration as well as covering any mark left by the icing.

To complete; a 'V' is cut into the ribbon when the exact length required has been determined (Fig. 68(e)). The ribbons are attached to the corners of the cake with a little icing.

SEWN BOW

It is not very easy to tie a ribbon round a cake. The band is never tight enough and tends to slip, thus spoiling the appearance. To overcome this, the band of ribbon is stuck firmly to the cake and the bow made separately to be stuck over the join later.

To determine the length of the band, a tape measure is placed around the cake and a piece of ribbon cut 1 cm ($\frac{1}{2}$ in) longer than the circumference. A bulb of icing, the same colour as the ribbon is piped on the front of the cake and one end of the band, right side facing outwards, placed into it. The ribbon is wrapped tightly around the cake and another bulb of icing is placed on the other end, thus sticking the ribbon firmly to the cake.

The previously made bow is stuck on top of the band with another bulb of icing, ensuring it conceals the overlap. Always use icing to stick ribbon and never be tempted to use pins which are less effective and most dangerous.

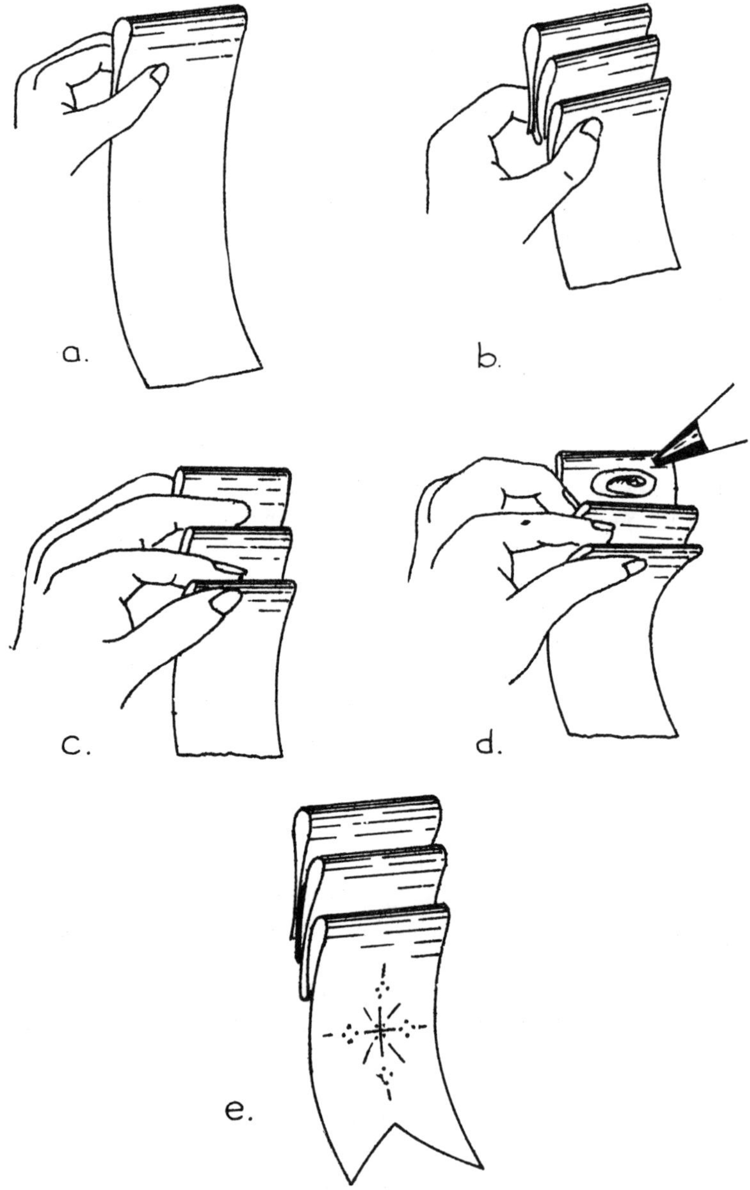

Fig. 68. The looped ribbon.

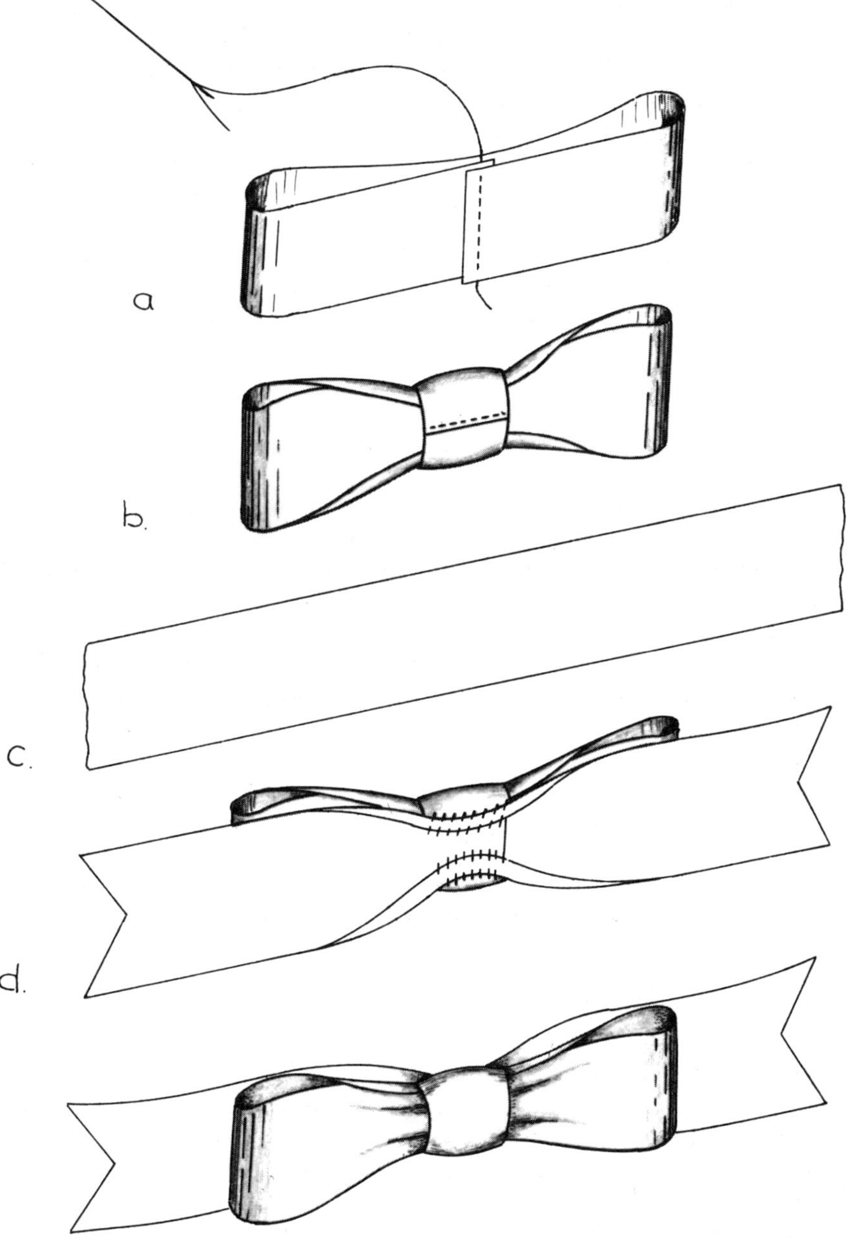

Fig. 69. The sewn bow.

The sewn bow is made as follows: Take a piece of ribbon 25 cm (10 in) long and form into a circle overlapping the ends by about 1 cm ($\frac{1}{2}$ in). Making sure that the join is in the middle of the ribbon, sew a row of running stitches through the three layers of ribbon and draw together before securing and cutting the thread (Fig. 69(a)).

A short piece of ribbon about 5 cm (2 in) long is placed around the centre of the bow and also sewn at the back. If the ribbon is quite wide, it is advisable to fold it in half in order to achieve a neat appearance (Fig. 69(b)).

To form the backpiece, a length of ribbon approximately 18 cm (7 in) long is required (Fig. 69(c)). This piece of ribbon is gathered in the middle and sewn on to the back of the bow. Finally a 'V' is cut in each end of the ribbon (Fig. 69(d)).

Edible Corner Decorations

These edible pieces are used mainly for the corners of square cakes. If a ribbon or bow is not required it is usual to decorate the sides of a cake in some other way. It has been seen that small runouts or piping can be carried out on the sides, but the corners tend to look unfinished without some adornment.

It is quite possible to pipe small shells down the corners, but for those wishing to do something different, here are two unusual types of corner pieces.

The first is a runout and the second a piped piece. Both are piped on to waxed paper and should be made in advance. They may be traced directly from the drawings in Fig. 70, but as the depth of cakes vary, they may require altering in order to achieve the correct size.

When using this type of decoration, the depth of the cake should be measured after it has been coated. This measurement should then be used for the corner pieces. If the cake is to have a top runout border, the corner piece should measure slightly less than the side of the cake in order for the piece to fit underneath it.

RUNOUT CORNER PIECE

Check that the design in Fig. 70 is suitable for the cake depth, and, following any adjustments, make six tracings on to a sheet of greaseproof paper. Place the tracings on to a board, cover with waxed paper, and secure the corners with a little icing.

With a No. 1 tube in a small bag of icing to piping consistency, outline the

Fig. 70. Drawings for edible corner pieces.

designs in the usual way. When all the outlines have been completed, the designs are flooded, quite thickly, using icing as stiff as possible for runout work. These are left under gentle heat for a few minutes before being left to dry in a moisture-free atmosphere.

Peel the runouts from the waxed paper when thoroughly dry, turn over, and place onto a clean piece of waxed paper. Using softened icing, flood the underside of the runout. It is not necessary to outline again with a No. 1 tube, but using a paint brush, take the icing to the outer edges and produce a neat finish. Leave to dry as previously explained.

During the drying process, this type of runout is apt to 'sink' a little, making a dent in the surface. This will be avoided if the consistency of the icing is as thick as possible. It must not flow from the bag, but be capable of being made smooth with the aid of a paint brush. To finish, an edging should be piped with a No. 1 or No. 0 tube. figure 71 illustrates the production of the runout.

PIPED CORNER PIECE

Because this is a very delicate piped scroll I suggest that in order to cover breakages you make twice as many pieces as you require (instead of just two spare ones as I have suggested for items previously described).

Place a piece of waxed paper over the drawing and make secure with a little icing. Put a No. 2 tube into a small bag and half fill with icing of piping

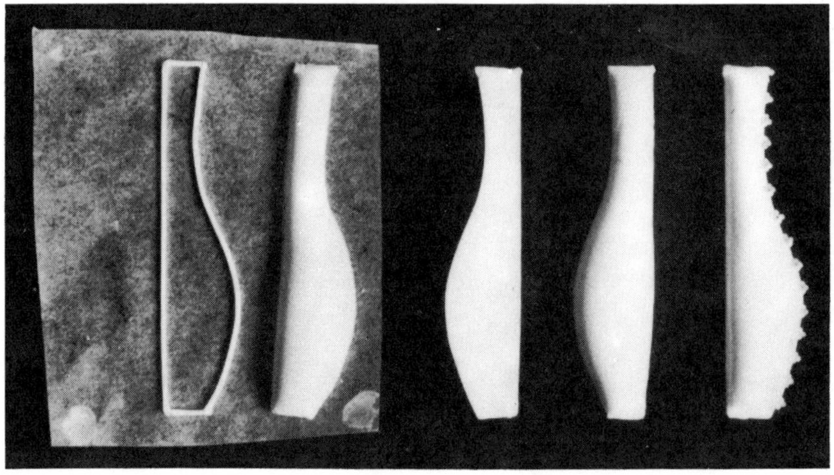

Fig. 71. Runout corner piece.

consistency. Using the touch, lift and place method, outline the scrolls, making sure that there are no gaps where the linework joins. When the icing has dried a little, overpipe the scrolls again, still using a No. 2 tube.

When crusted, a second layer of overpiping is carried out using a No. 1 tube. Instead of plain linework this overpiping is made with a small shell or 'push and pull' action. Care must be taken to see that every section is joined, otherwise the design would not hold together when removed from the paper. At this stage the design must be left for several hours to dry thoroughly.

When absolutely dry, a small palette knife is placed *very gently* underneath the piping to separate the scroll from the paper. It is then carefully turned over and placed on to a clean piece of waxed paper, in preparation for the overpiping to be repeated. The corner piece is completed with a No. 1 shell on the reverse side of the scroll. Figure 72 illustrates the four stages of piping.

TO ASSEMBLE CORNER PIECES

Both types are held in position on the cake by placing a small amount of icing from a No. 1 tube where the corner piece touches the cake. A paint brush is used to remove any surplus icing.

If the bottom border is to be piped, the corners are assembled at the same time as the border is carried out. If a flooded border is to be used, the bottom border should be flooded and the corners placed into position before

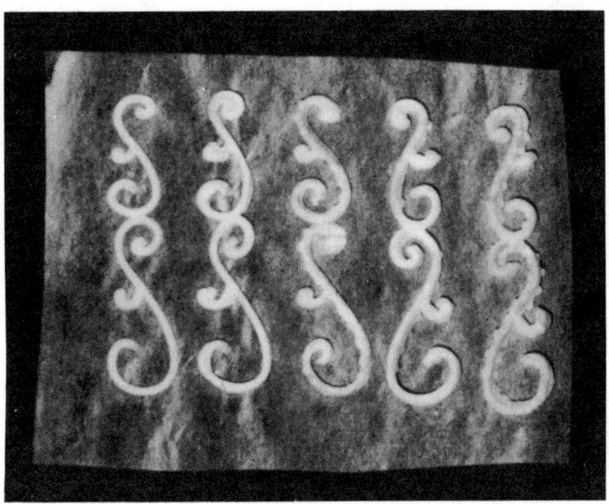

Fig. 72. Piped corner piece.

the icing is completely dry. This ensures that the corner is firmly held in place.

If preferred, the corners may be placed on top of the flooded bottom border, in which case the border must be absolutely dry before this can be done. Also, an allowance will have to be made for the depth of icing on the board when measuring the depth of the cake.

Runout corner pieces are shown on the dummy in Figs. 61 and 63, Chapter 9.

Chapter 12

Marzipan Roses

Many flowers, fruit and animals can be modelled from marzipan, but for use as decoration on royal iced cakes, the rose is the most acceptable because of its delicate appearance and universal appeal.

If possible, 'natural' marzipan should be used for modelling but if this is not available a good quality golden marzipan can be used. Almond paste is not suitable because of its coarse texture. The disadvantage of using golden marzipan is its basic yellow colour which combines with any colouring additive to give a secondary colour. It is impossible to achieve a delicate pink for example, and the delightful shades and harmony that can be achieved by colouring natural marzipan are unobtainable. The golden marzipan can only effectively be used with a white cake, when any distortion in the colours is not easily discernible. Although rich red roses can be made from natural marzipan, they only look their best when used on a white cake.

Paste colouring is often used to avoid the marzipan becoming sticky, but in the majority of cases liquid colouring is quite acceptable unless a colour of great depth is required, as with deep red roses.

Marzipan is very expensive and should be used with care. It must be kept wrapped in polythene at all times to prevent a crust forming, which would make it unsuitable for modelling.

Very little equipment is required to produce roses or leaves; the only requirements being a small polythene bag, a small board or tray, a quantity of suitable colouring and a small, sharp knife. A clean, damp dishcloth may be required should the hands become sticky.

Making the Rose

After a little practice, modelling roses becomes very satisfying and makes a welcome change from the routine of icing. Before commencing, ensure the hands have been well washed because the marzipan will be frequently handled.

The marzipan is prepared by folding in the colour with the fingers, taking care not to knead the paste or the oil will come to the surface making it difficult to handle. When the desired shade has been reached and no streaks of colour are showing, it should be wrapped in polythene to prevent any crusting. Only the small amount required for a petal is removed at any one time.

1. Take a small amount of coloured marzipan and roll into a ball about the size of a glacé cherry. The top of the ball is then gently pinched between the finger and thumb and formed into a cone. Place the cone down on a clean surface, to be used later as the centre of the rose. The size of ball determines the size of the rose; a larger ball for a big rose and smaller one for a small rose (Fig. 73).

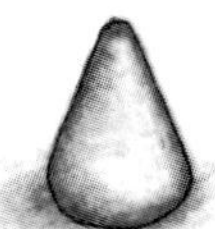

Fig. 73.

2. The petals are formed from another ball of marzipan of a similar size to that used for the centre. The ball is placed into a clean polythene bag, and with the index finger on top of the bag, the ball is pressed into a disc of an even thickness, about the depth of a lp piece. Approximately three quarters of the circumference for about 4 mm ($\frac{1}{8}$ in) from the edge of the marzipan is pressed to a fine edge. This tapered section is used to form the curl of the petal and if it is tapered excessively, the edge will lose its shape when assembled on the rose (Figs. 74 and 75).

3. With the cone in one hand and the petal in the other, wrap the petal around the cone, the thick part of the petal being placed at the base of the cone (Fig. 76).

4. When the petal has been wrapped around the cone the point of the cone should not be visible and the top of the petal should form a small opening (Fig. 77).

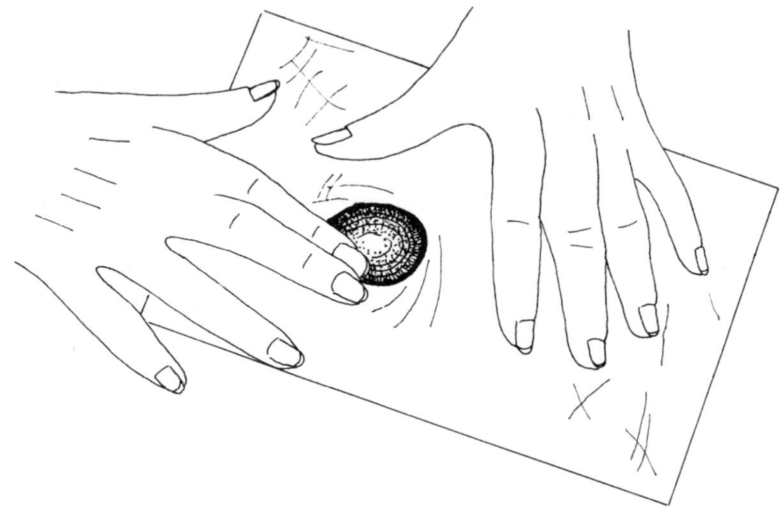

Fig. 74.

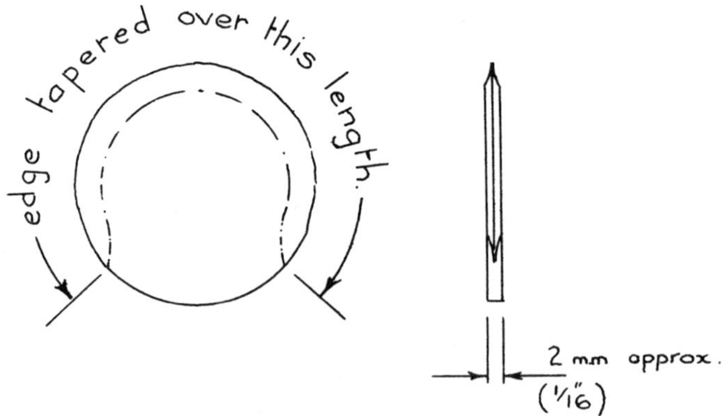

Fig. 75.

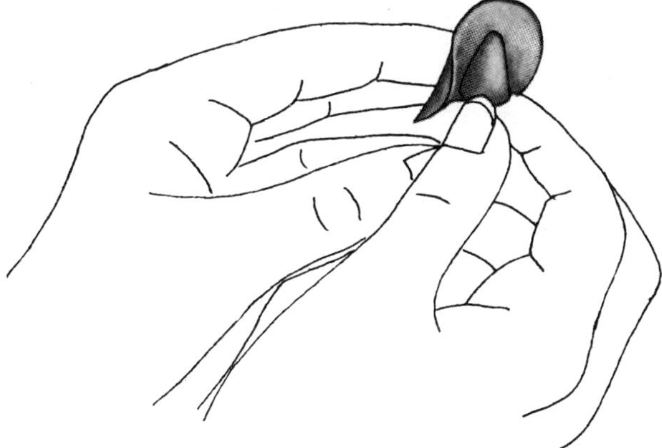

Fig. 76.

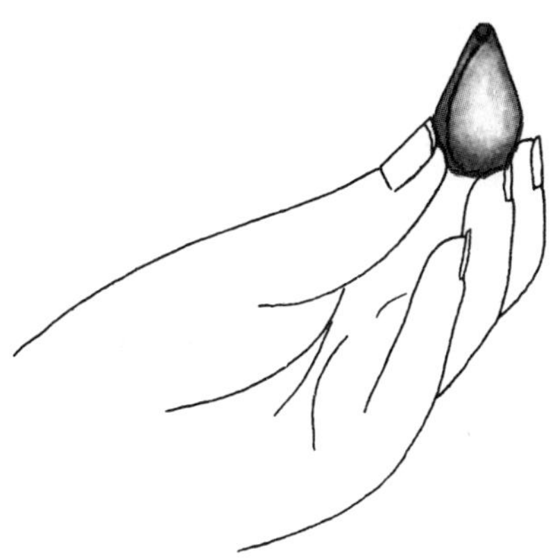

Fig. 77.

5. Press out another petal keeping the base and middle thick, whilst three quarters of the outer edge is quite thin. Mould the petal around the thumb to produce a 'cupped' shape, and gently curl back the top of the petal with the finger to produce a realistic effect (Fig. 78).

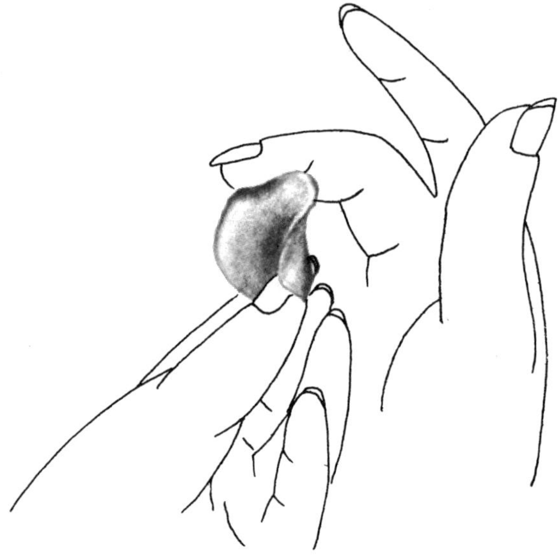

Fig. 78.

6. This petal is placed on the cone, over the joint, and should be slightly higher than the cone. When one stage has been completed, always stand the rose on a board whilst modelling the next petal. This ensures that the completed rose will sit correctly on the cake (Fig. 79).

Fig. 79.

7. Another petal is made in a similar way and placed opposite the previous one (Fig. 80). When the rose is put on to the board it will be seen

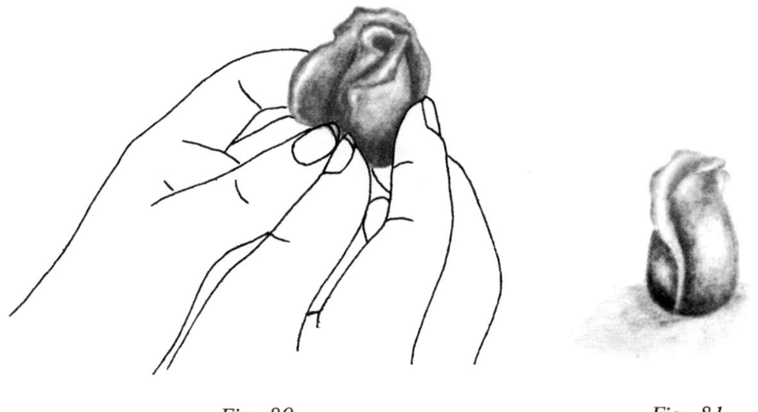

Fig. 80. *Fig. 81.*

that it now forms a bud. Curl the petals a little more if necessary, whilst the marzipan is still soft (Fig. 81).

8. Having formed the bud, three more petals are added to make it into a small rose. Mould them in exactly the same way as previously described and add them one at a time to the bud. Put the first petal in position and adjust the shape with a finger as required. Place the second petal inside the first and not around it; this being the main difference from making the bud. The third petal is placed inside the second (Fig. 82).

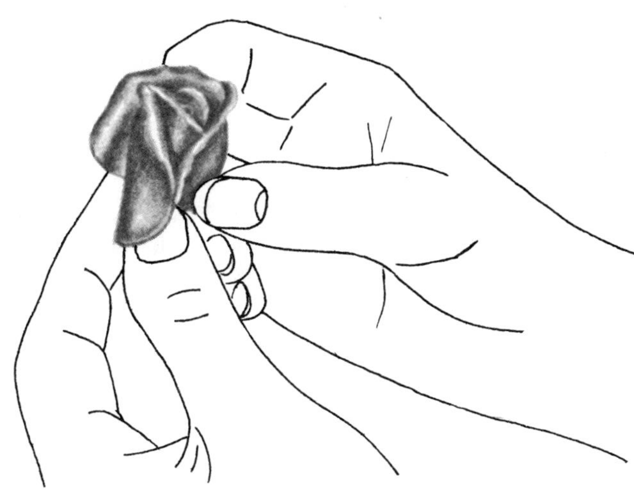

Fig. 82.

9. A small rose is now formed and can be used as such. When placed on the board, any final adjustments can be made to the curl of the petals (Fig. 83).

10. If a larger rose is required, four more additional petals are added in a similar way. Each petal is inserted inside the previous one but placed in a slightly lower position to give the open effect. Additional curl on the edges adds to the realism (Fig. 84).

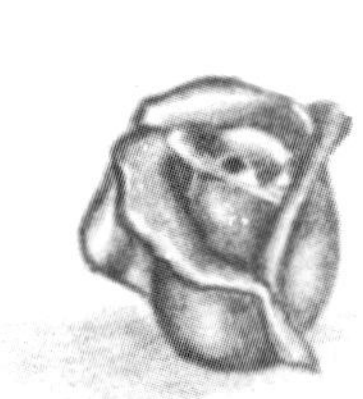

Fig. 83.

Fig. 84.

A common fault is making the outer edge of the petal too thin so that it falls back instead of bending gracefully. However, if the edge is too thick, the rose will appear clumsy. Practice is required to achieve the correct thickness.

If the rose looks like a cabbage, it is because the petals are not being placed high enough. When a rose is nearing completion, lower the petals and even have them almost falling away, but not in the initial stages.

Do not make every rose in full bloom. Buds and small roses will also be required; a spray of roses all the same shape and size will not look realistic.

Once a rose has been made to satisfaction, experiment by adding more petals or by letting a petal fall away from a completed bud to produce a natural effect.

Red roses should be a deep rich red. Roses in pale colours may be shaded, and this is very attractive and easy to accomplish. If a pink rose is required, three shades of pink marzipan are made; the deepest shade being used for the centre and the bud, a slightly lighter shade for the next three petals and a very light pink for the last four. Needless to say, the same colouring must be used for each shade. Figure 85 shows each stage of making a rose.

Fig. 85.

Making the Leaves

These are simple and straight forward to make. Only a very small amount of marzipan will be required and should be coloured green.

If an aerograph is available and the finished leaves are sprayed with a little brown colouring, the result is very realistic. However, as most people do not have such a gadget, the next best thing is to add a very small amount of brown marzipan to the green and fold it in until the green becomes speckled with brown.

Take a ball of green marzipan, half the size of the one used for the rose. Form into a small cone and place inside a polythene bag. Press out evenly, but not too thinly, to form the shape of a leaf. Without removing it from the bag, draw the veins on the leaf with the knife. Remove from the bag and pinch the wide part of the leaf so that it bends a little (Fig. 86). Place on to a sheet of greaseproof paper until set.

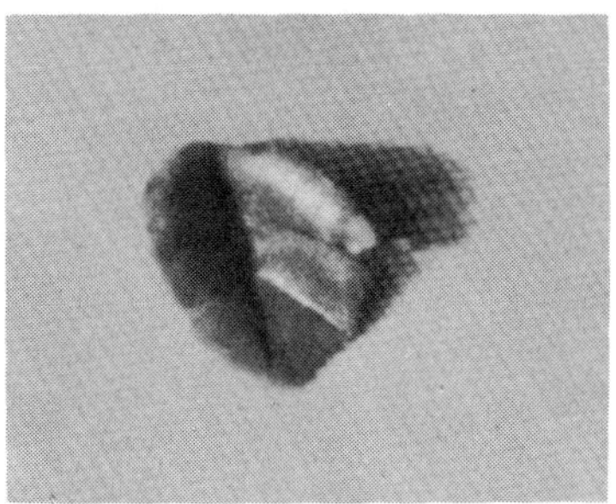

Fig. 86. Marzipan leaf.

Do not attempt to make every leaf the same. Make some large and some very small by adjusting the size of the marzipan ball. Some may be left over the handle of a spoon in order that they dry curved.

Roses and leaves will be very soft and easily damaged until they have dried out. Always make them several days in advance, if possible.

Marzipan roses will keep for a long time, but they do become hard unless brushed with a little cocoa butter melted to blood heat. To avoid them being damaged, they can be stored in egg boxes.

Assembling roses and leaves will be covered in Chapter 15 (see Fig. 154).

Chapter 13

Advanced Runouts and Figure Piping

The basic principles of runout work are explained in Chapter 9 and only a few additional details need to be known for the more intricate designs, i.e. designs where several sections are necessary to complete one figure.

Water Lily

All the petals required for the water lily are the same as used for the marguerite (Fig. 59, Chapter 9) but the disc is larger. One petal and the disc are shown in Fig. 87.

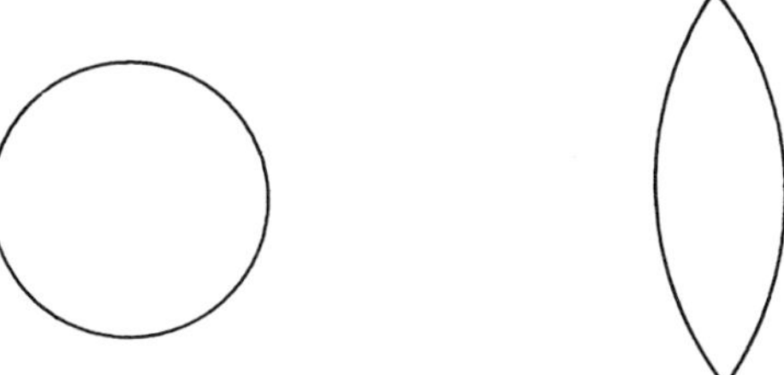

Fig. 87. Drawing for water lily disc and petal.

Instead of the one set of petals as required for the marguerite, the water lily has three sets. As eight petals are required for each set and ten are recommended to be made to cover breakages, a total of thirty petals is required.

All the petals are runout as described for the marguerite, but the first set is *dried flat*. The second ten petals are *dried on a curved dish* similar to the marguerite petals. The third batch are *dried on a roller* to increase the amount of curvature. A wooden or metal roller is ideal (see Fig. 90, Chapter 13), but a cardboard roll from the inside of a container of tin foil is adequate.

When the disc and petals are completely dry, they are assembled as follows:

1. Place the disc in the centre of the cake, or in the required position and stick down with a little icing. The disc is not raised from the surface, as the petals for a water lily are placed on top of the disc. (The marguerite petals have to be placed underneath the disc.)
2. Secure eight flat petals, equal distance apart, on to the outer edge of the disc with a little icing.
3. In the space between the flat petals, secure the curved petals (ones formed in the dish) on to the disc, with the tips curving inwards. A little cotton wool may be required to hold them in position.
4. Finally, secure the petals from the roller so that they also curve inwards to form an inner ring of petals. A little icing flooded into the centre of the petals will form the middle of the flower.
5. When the icing is dry, stamens similar to the ones on the marguerite may be piped.

Figure 88 shows a completed water lily.

Curved Leaves

These are also placed on a roller to dry and can be used for the outer edge of a cake, forming part of a runout top border (Fig. 153, Chapter 15). Each leaf requires a support which is flooded and dried flat. Figure 89 provides the working drawing for the leaf and support.

The leaf is outlined on to waxed paper with a No. 1 tube, and filigree is piped with a No. 0 tube. The leaf is flooded as quickly as possible and placed on to the roller to dry curved, secured in position with a little icing. The leaf should be flooded sparingly to avoid the shape becoming distorted when placed on the roller. More leaves than required should be made to allow for breakages. An edging may be piped, if required, when dry.

The leaves are assembled by securing the flat edge of the support on to the edge of the cake. When this has set, a little icing is placed under both ends of the leaf and it is gently placed over the edge of the cake. The tip of the leaf should rest on the pointed edge of the support and the wide edge

Fig. 88. Completed water lily.

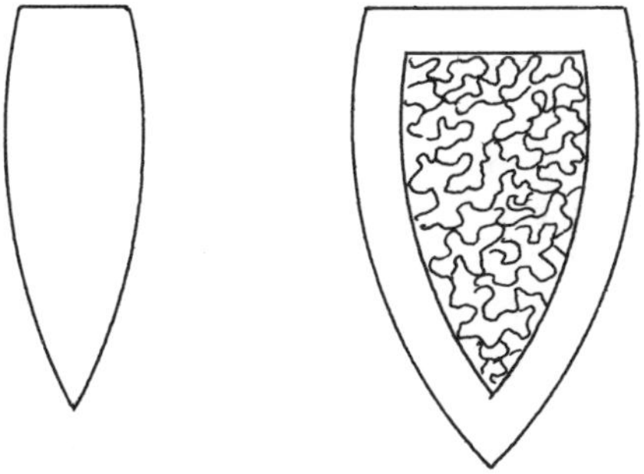

Fig. 89. Drawing of support and leaf.

Fig. 90. Petals and leaves on a roller.

immediately behind the flat edge of the support. Figure 90 shows leaves and petals on a roller and Fig. 91 indicates the positioning of a leaf on a support.

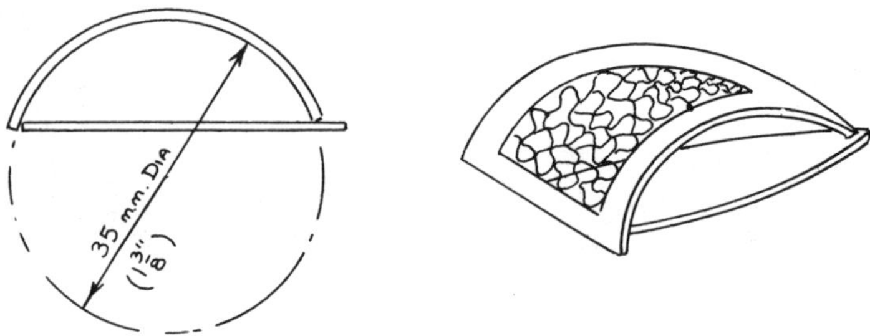

Fig. 91. Positioning leaf on support.

Animal and Human Form

Human faces are difficult to reproduce in icing and the best way of achieving success is to avoid them! When looking for designs choose the ones with a profile or where the face is hidden by a hat. If a face must be shown, it should be painted very carefully on the dried runout with a very fine sable-hair paint brush. The faces of animals do not present the same difficulty as it is not essential they are copied with the same degree of accuracy. Figure 92 shows greetings cards chosen for runout purposes.

It is not essential that the whole design is reproduced and often only part of the design is required. An example of this is the little girl in Fig. 106,

Fig. 92. Greetings cards used for runouts.

Chapter 13. This drawing was taken from a sheet of gift wrapping paper and formed part of a large design. It has been used with or without the basket. A string of balloons has been used to replace the flowers in her hand and the dress has been decorated in many different ways.

The design should be studied very carefully before icing takes place. It will be seen that some parts of the runout need to be thicker than others to give realism. A sleeve, for instance, needs to look as though it is on top of an arm. To give correct form, the arm is runout and the sleeve runout over the top of it. This increases the thickness at the correct point and avoids the runout lacking definition.

When piping the human form, always start with the face and as many other parts as can be done without coming into contact with another section. Flooding an adjoining part before one has crusted would cause them to merge into each other. If some portion of a completed runout does not give the required thickness, the area can be flooded again.

RUNOUT FIGURES

Runout figures are usually small and therefore small bags of icing are used. If they require outlining (and not many do) use a No. 1 tube with icing of piping consistency and the same colour as for the flooding.

Dilute the remaining icing, and colour very small amounts making sure that every colour required is available in small bags before commencing work. The hole cut in the bags should not be larger than that in a No. 2 tube. Figure 93 shows the way in which a runout is completed. Note that although delicate, this runout is not outlined. The consistency of the icing needs to be as thick as possible in order that it will stay where required.

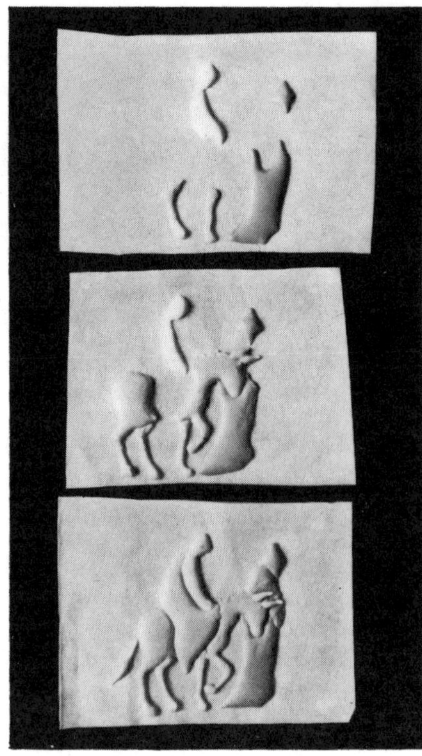

Fig. 93. Completion of runout figures (three stages).

PROMINENT FEATURES

Sometimes a part of a runout needs to be very prominent. Two such examples are the cheeks of a child and, as illustrated in Fig. 158, Chapter 15, the baby's form underneath the covering.

Cheeks are made by placing a small bulb of icing over the required place. It is left to dry for a few moments and then the rest of the face, including the cheeks, are flooded. This will give a plump realistic effect to the cheeks. The same procedure was followed for the baby in Fig. 158. Before flooding for the blanket, I placed a bulb of icing where I imagined the baby's body would be. After it had crusted, the blanket was flooded over the bulb of icing and the correct effect was achieved.

FLESH COLOUR

Flesh colour is obtained by mixing a small amount of pink with an even smaller amount of yellow. Only a very little icing is required and the colour, when wet, should appear off-white in order to dry flesh pink.

PAINTING RUNOUTS

Painting completed runouts is quite usual, but they must be absolutely dry. Hair can be runout in a paler shade than required and then 'streaked' with the correct colour using a fine paint brush. A little extra colour may be needed on a face and this must be done with great care. In Fig. 94 the hooves and features were painted on the donkey after the runout had dried. The inside of the ears, the eye and the muzzle were flooded white. The remainder of the donkey was flooded pale brown and streaked with brown colouring using a fine paint brush.

PIPING ON RUNOUTS

Piping may be applied on top of a dry runout. This is often in the form of flowers or additional decoration to a dress. Such decoration is always carried out with a No. 0 tube. Figure 95 shows a runout on to which a basket of flowers and other decoration has been piped. Ringlets underneath the bonnet and flowers in the hand cannot be piped until the runout has been placed on to the cake.

FREEHAND PIPING

Freehand piping is often used for garden scenes. Crazy paving, grass, flowers and even a tree can be piped directly on to the surface. Do not be afraid when piping these objects as no definite pattern is required and no two trees are alike! Always use a No. 0 tube and dark brown icing for paving and trees. Do not use the touch, lift and place method, but touch the

Fig. 94. Painting runouts.

surface with the tube. Foliage can be applied with a No. 0 tube and green icing or with green colouring and a paint brush. When painting, care must be taken to have the brush as dry as possible. Additional piping in the form of blossom and the like can be carried out with a No. 0 tube. Figures 146, 149 and 152, Chapter 15, illustrate freehand piping combined with runouts.

Fig. 95. Piping on runouts.

Figure Piping

Small figures can, after practice, be piped without the aid of drawings. It is possible to pipe them directly on to the cake surface but until they have been perfected it is preferable to pipe them on waxed paper.

The consistency of the icing for figure piping is only slightly softer than that used for piping shells and linework. It is not necessary to let one section crust before adding another.

Figure 96 shows some elementary figures and the way in which they were piped. These figures were all piped with a No. 3 tube, but eyes, feet and tails, etc. were added with a No. 1 tube. In the case of the lambs and kittens the fur effect was achieved by adding dots of icing with a No. 0 tube after the original piping had dried.

Plain tubes are used and correct pressure is important in figure piping. Where large bulbs are required, the icing must be piped boldly. The same tube can be used for smaller parts by using less pressure.

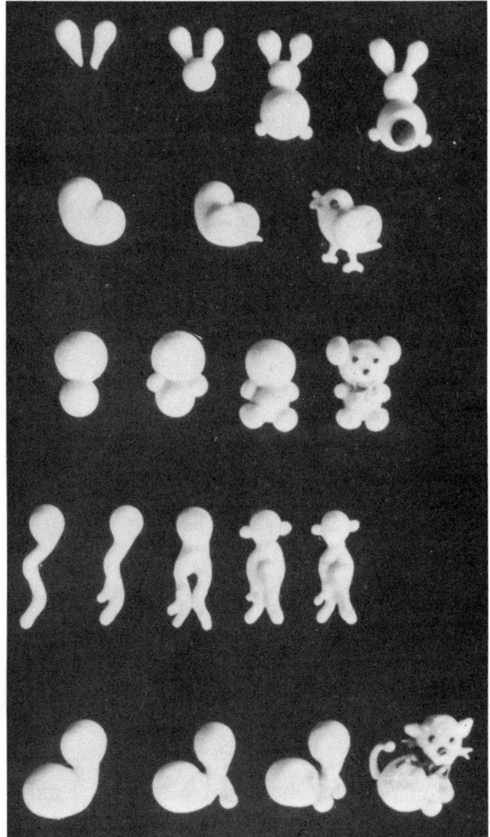

Fig. 96. Figure piping.

The following pages contain many drawings for runouts that can be traced from the book. All of them have been successfully used and will form a good basis to develop further ideas (Figs. 97–109).

Fig. 97.

Fig. 98.

Fig. 99.

Fig. 100.

Fig. 101.

Fig. 102.

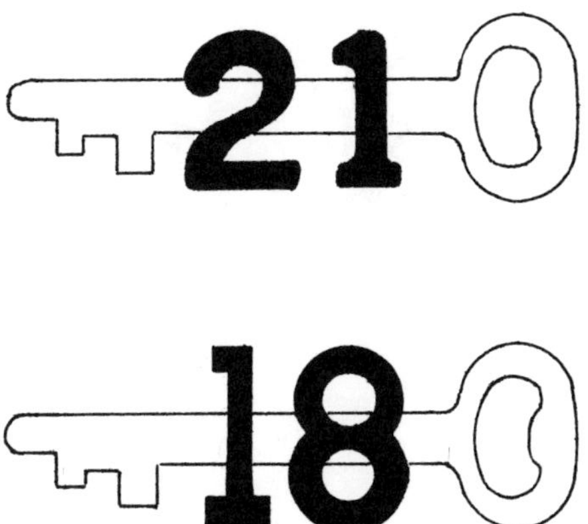

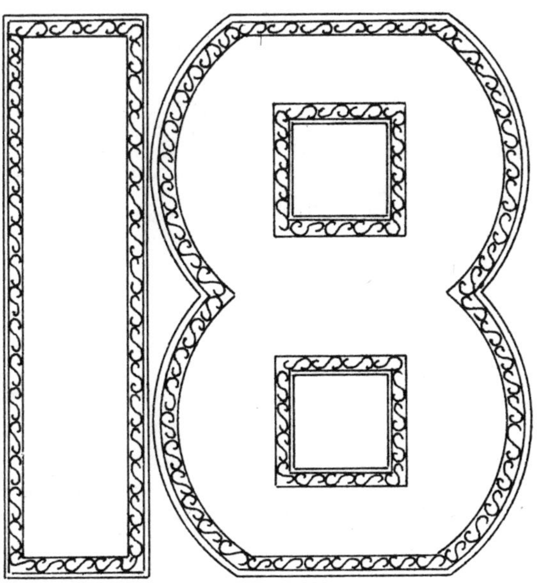

Fig. 103.

Fig. 104.

Fig. 105.

Fig. 106.

Fig. 107.

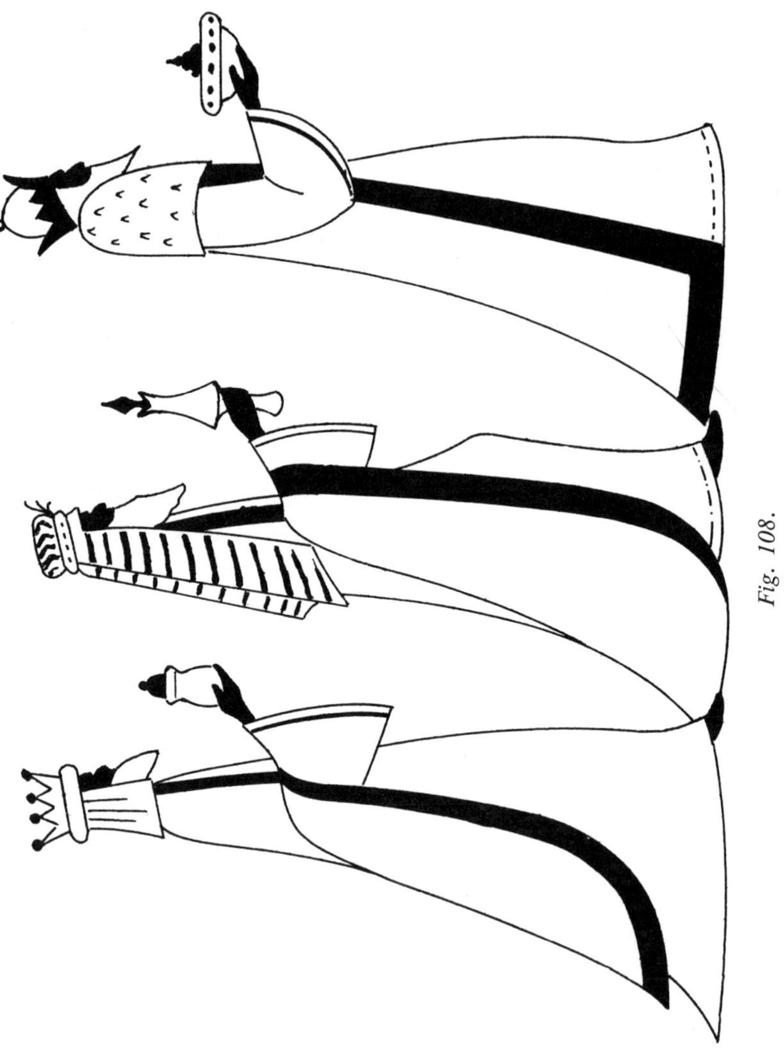

Fig. 108.

Fig. 109.

Chapter 14

Runout Borders

There are two types of runout borders; a continuous band or 'collar', illustrated in Fig. 110 (round) and Fig. 111 (square), or runout 'pieces' as illustrated in Fig. 112 (round) and Fig. 113 (square).

Both types are suitable for round or square cakes, though it will be found easier to make separate pieces and assemble them on the cake rather than the collar which is made in one piece. Not only are the pieces easier to

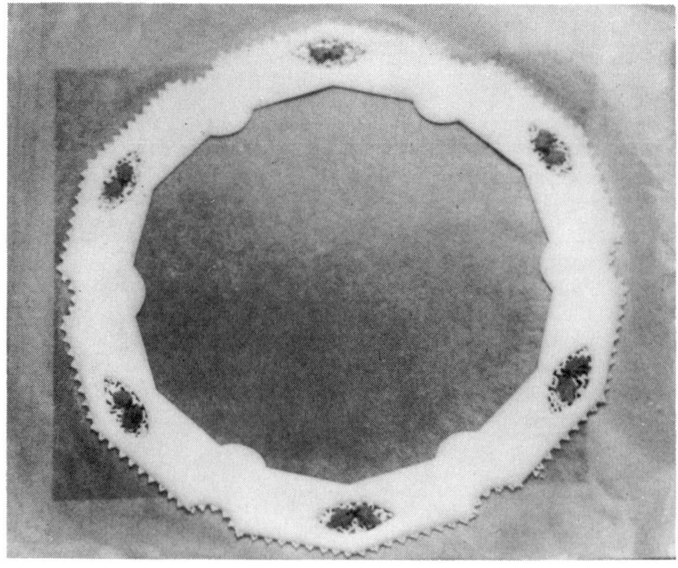

Fig. 110. Round collar.

execute, they are less fragile than the larger collar. Collars are unsuitable for very large cakes as their size makes them impractical.

Fig. 111. Square collar.

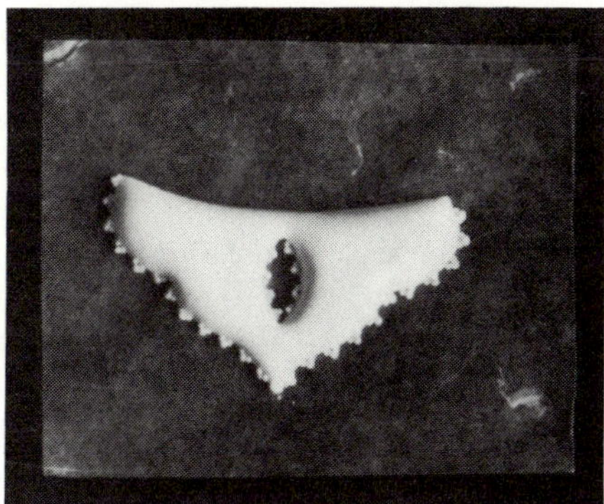

Fig. 112. Runout piece for a round cake.

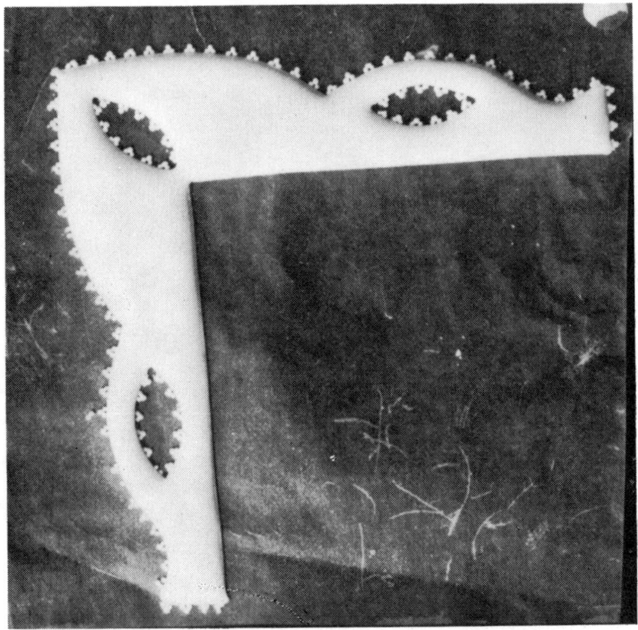

Fig. 113. Runout piece for a square cake.

Bottom Borders

To give a balanced appearance it is essential that a cake with a runout top border should have a flooded bottom border, and these have been covered in Chapter 7.

The reader will recall that in Chapter 2, I recommended that a cake with a piped border should have a board 5 cm (2 in) greater in diameter than the cake itself. In the case of a cake with a runout border, the cake board should be 8–10 cm (3–4 in) greater in diameter than the cake to prevent the cake from looking 'top heavy'.

The flooded border may be a plain one as described in Chapter 7, but it is also possible to flood the bottom board to match the runout on top (see Fig. 125). For this a template is required which can be placed on the board and outlined with a No. 1 tube. The template is then removed and the board flooded. It is also possible to draw the design in pencil on the cake board before the cake is placed on to the board. As this border is flooded directly on to the cake board icing containing glycerine can be used.

How to Design a Runout Border

To prepare your design you will need a large sheet of drawing paper, a flat working surface, a pair of compasses, a ruler, a pencil and a rubber. Instructions are given on how to design runout borders, but some have been drawn and can be traced directly from this book. However, to enable the illustrations to be printed full size and capable of being traced for actual runout work, some of them show only part of the runout.

On square corner pieces the design is repeated on each leg. By tracing the illustration and turning the paper over, the other part can be traced in position on the other side, thus showing the complete design.

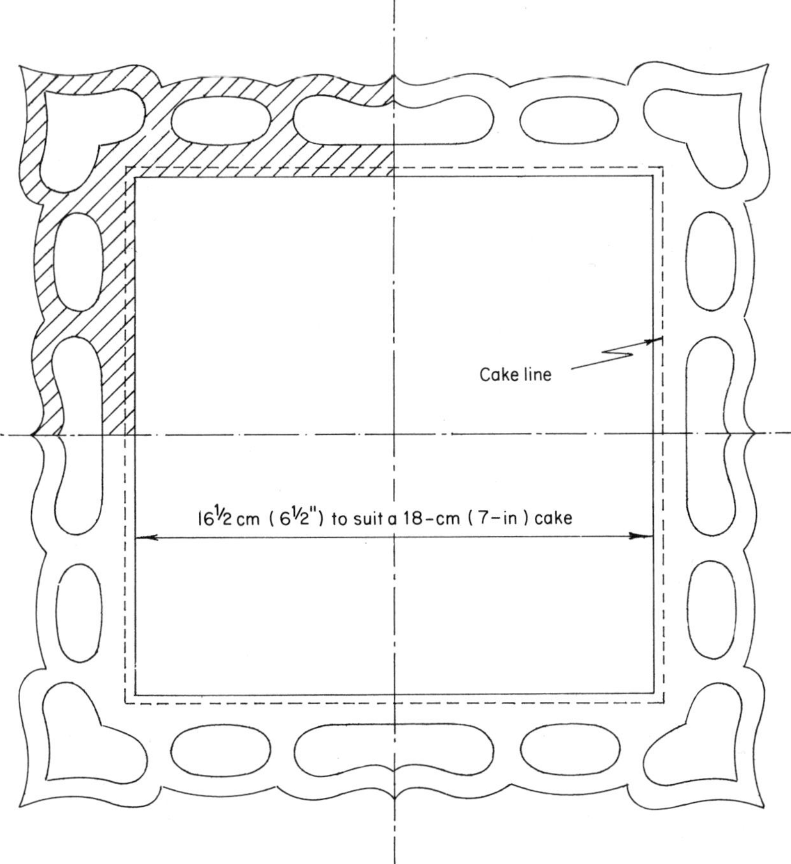

Fig. 114. Design for a square collar.

Only a section of each collar design has been shown. If the inside ring or square is drawn 1 cm ($\frac{1}{2}$ in) smaller than the size of the cake, the design can be traced in sections around it. Figure 114 shows a completed runout drawing built up in this way. When designing runout collars or pieces to fit a round cake it is advantageous to be able to divide a circle into equal parts. This enables the patterns to be drawn with a degree of accuracy that ensures all the runouts will fit their intended position. Also, with all the runouts being of a similar size, the finished cake will have a well-balanced look.

One of the most popular and easiest to do is to divide a circle into six. This is carried out by drawing a circle with compasses. From point 1 step off the radius to get points 6, 2, 3 and 4. Return to point 6 and strike off point 5. By carrying out in this order any error is reduced (Fig. 115).

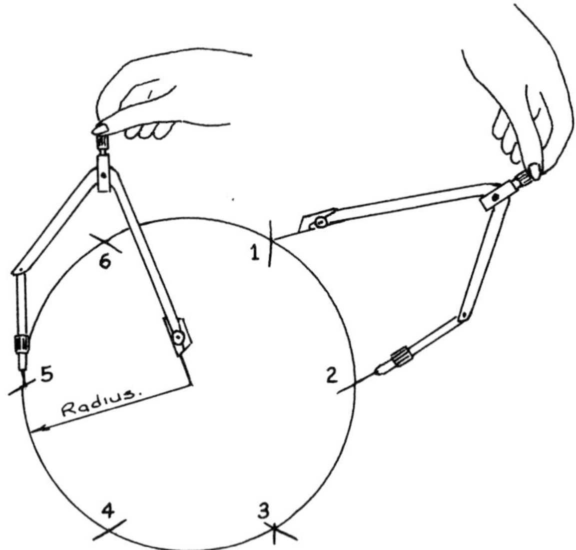

Fig. 115. Dividing a circle into six.

Having been divided into six, the circle can easily be further subdivided into twelve. By striking off two arcs from points 1 and 2 and by drawing a line from where they cross to the centre of the circle and extending it to the opposite edge, two of the six sectors will each be divided into two equal parts. Similar treatment to two of the other sectors will divide the circle into twelve equal parts (Fig. 116).

Another popular choice is eight divisions. To do this, draw a line through the centre of the circle. From points 1 and 2 strike off two arcs to cross at

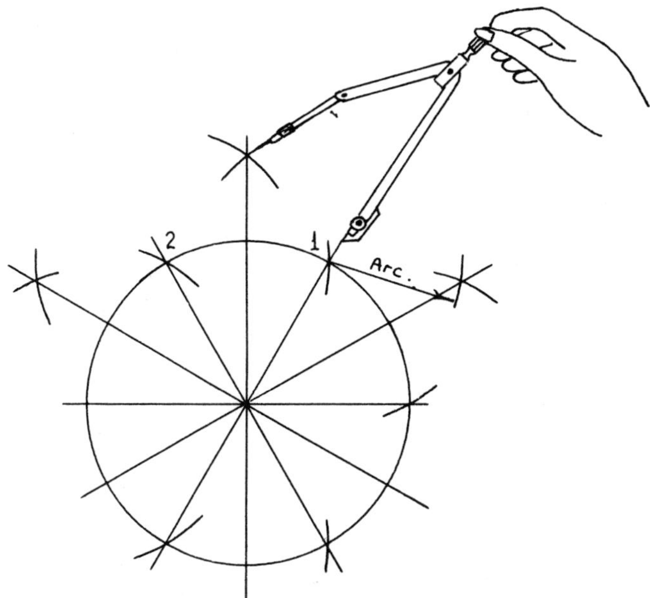

Fig. 116. Dividing a circle into twelve.

point 3. A line from point 3 through the centre to the further edge of the circle will divide it into four equal parts. Similar subdivisions from points 1 and 4 and 4 and 2 will divide the circle into eight equal parts (Fig. 117).

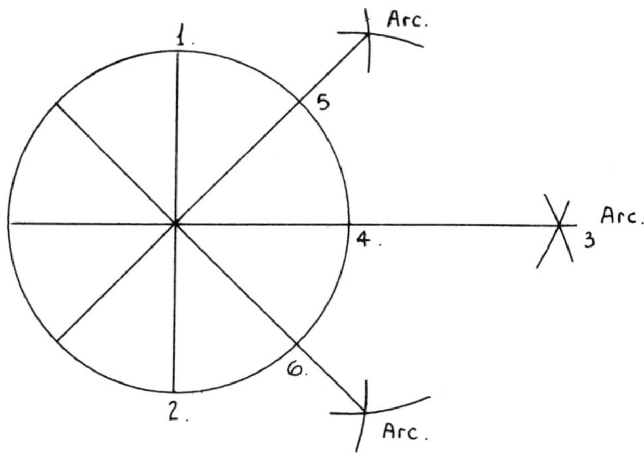

Fig. 117. Dividing a circle into eight.

Having drawn a circle and divided it into various sectors it is now a relatively simple matter to design a collar for a round cake.

1. Measure the diameter of the top of the cake and set the compasses to half this size and draw a circle. This is known as the cake line.
2. Draw another circle 1 cm ($\frac{1}{2}$ in) less than the size of the cake. This inner ring ensures the collar has adequate support on the cake.
3. Draw an outer circle between 2 and 3 cm (1 and $1\frac{1}{2}$ in) greater to give the desired collar width.
4. Divide the outer circle into as many sectors as desired (Figs. 115–117).
5. Draw a design in one sector; this may require the sector to be subdivided in order to obtain a centre line (Fig. 118).
6. Repeat this design in the other sectors by drawing or tracing.

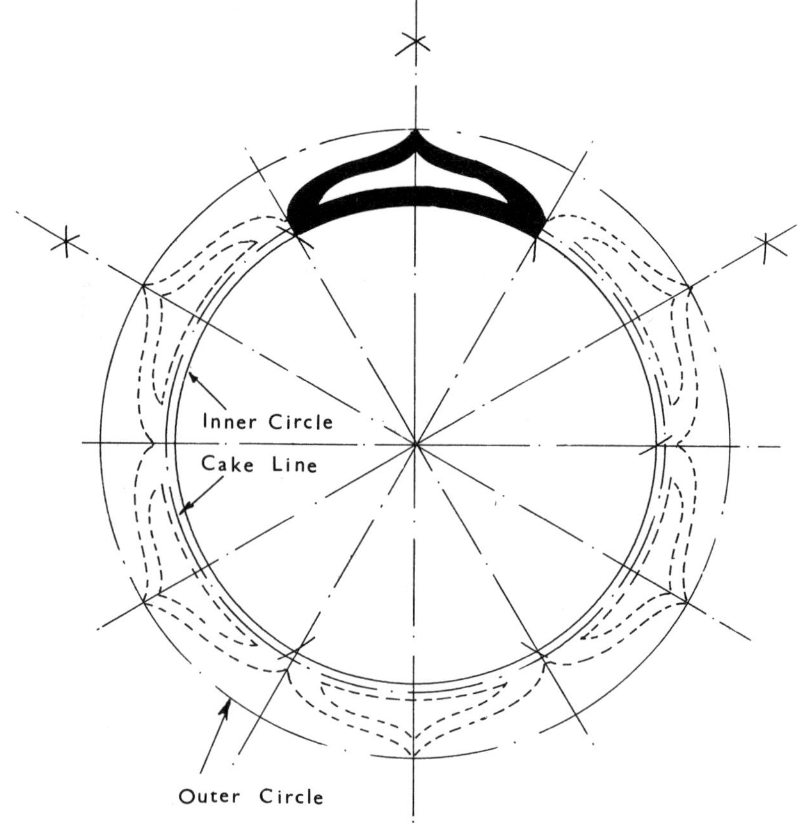

Fig. 118. How to design a round collar.

When designing separate runout pieces only one sector needs to be designed. The drawing should not completely fill the sector (see Fig. 138) as an allowance should be made for an edging or additional piping which is done after completion.

How to Execute Runout Borders

Runout collars and pieces are executed in the same way as other runouts and the same equipment is required. Waxed paper for collars and large pieces should be quite strong, but still thin enough for the design to be visible through it. The board or glass on to which the border is piped must be absolutely flat.

Collars and pieces are *always outlined with a No. 1 tube*. Large bags are required for the softened icing which must not contain glycerine. It is usual for runout borders to be the same colour as the cake coating.

Runout borders are best made from albumen or a fortified albumen solution rather than fresh egg whites. Experiments have shown that large runouts made with fresh egg whites do not always dry out sufficiently, although small runouts are quite satisfactory. The advantage of using powdered albumen is that the solution can be made as strong as desired.

Icing used for flooding should be left for several hours before use to disperse the air bubbles. Always make more pieces than required and two collars instead of one. If, hopefully, none gets broken, the spare pieces can be used another time.

A separate drawing is required for each runout and these tracings should clearly indicate the size of cake for which they are intended. Afterwards they should be put away and kept for future use.

When making a runout collar, round or square, first cut a cross in the centre of the waxed paper. This will avoid any damage to the runout should the paper contract whilst drying.

The procedure for making a runout collar or piece is as follows:

1. Place the drawings on a flat board and stick down with a little icing.
2. Place uncreased waxed paper, shiny side up, on top of the drawings and secure with a little icing. If a collar is being made, the paper should be cut in the middle in order to allow for expansion.
3. Put a No. 1 tube into a small bag and half fill with icing of piping consistency. If filigree work is also required a No. 0 tube will be needed as well. All icing used must be of the same colour.
4. Have ready several large bags half filled with softened icing. This may

be softer than that used for the figures as the outline will keep it from flowing too freely. It should not be too soft, however, otherwise the icing might 'sink' whilst drying. Always have more bags of icing than you think will be required in case of accidents.

5. Outline the runouts with a No. 1 tube (Fig. 119), making quite sure that there are no gaps where the icing could seep through.

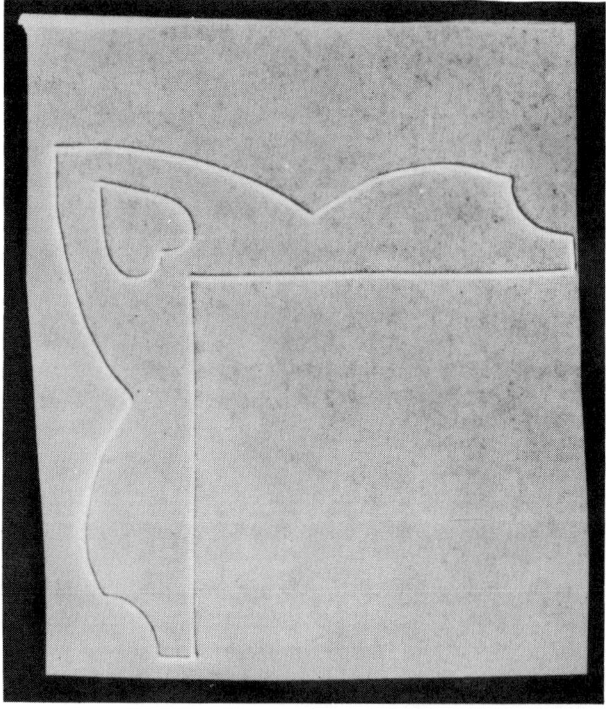

Fig. 119. Piped outline for corner piece.

6. If filigree is to be piped, it should be done at this stage with a No. 0 tube. This does not apply to any edging which is done after the runouts are completed and when they are quite dry. Filigree linework inside runouts must touch the outline and have no breaks, otherwise it would not hold together when removed from the waxed paper.

7. Take a large bag of icing and cut a hole about the size of a No. 3 tube. Flood the runout evenly using a fine paint brush to assist the icing into the corners and to cover the outline. If a collar is being executed only about three inches of icing should be flooded at one time. Immediately this has

been made smooth, another portion should be added to it starting at the other side. Alternate portions are added in this way until the band is complete. This avoids any part of the collar crusting before the adjoining section is flooded (Fig. 120).

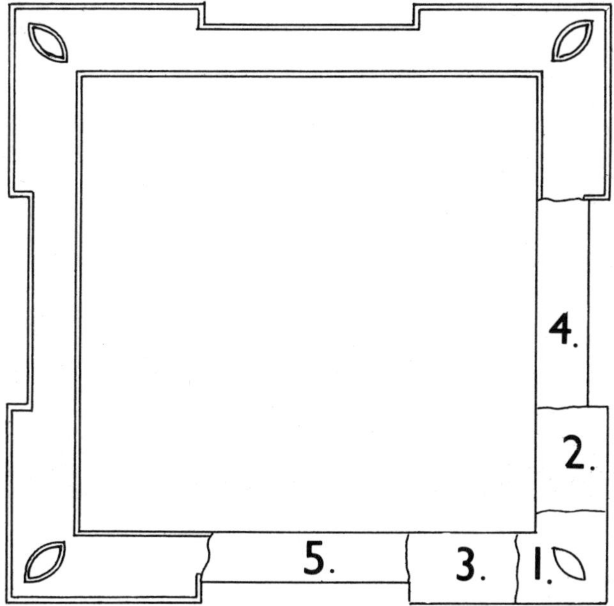

Fig. 120. Flooding a collar.

8. If several runouts are on one board, flood each one before placing them under a gentle heat. Whilst these are crusting, another batch can be executed. Place in a warm dry atmosphere for several days to dry.

9. Any edging required is piped on the dry runout before it is placed on the cake, but the runout may be loosened from the waxed paper before the piping takes place. This does not apply to plaques which are placed in the centre of a cake, making it easy to pipe an edging after the plaque has been assembled. Any edging that is broken when lifted from the waxed paper can be repaired when on the cake, but the firm surface of the board makes piping much easier to carry out before the runout is removed (Fig. 121).

NETTING

It has been seen that filigree linework can be piped inside runouts before flooding takes place. It is also possible to leave any inside design empty and

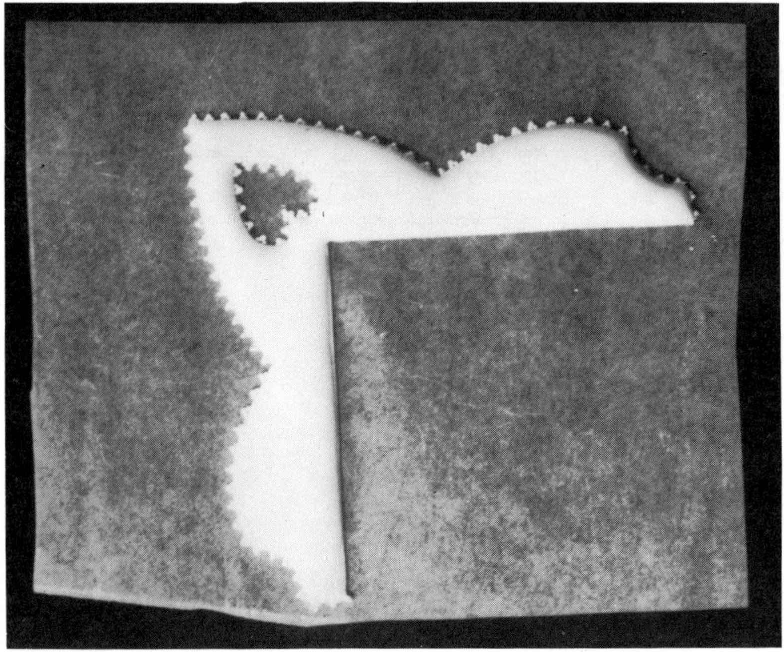

Fig. 121. Completed runout corner piece.

pipe an edging, similar to the outside edging, after the runout has dried (Fig. 121). Another form of ornamentation is netting; to do this the part to be piped is left empty until the runout has dried.

After the runout is dry an edging is piped and when this is also dry, the runout is peeled from the waxed paper and turned over. The netting is piped with a No. 1 tube on the back of the runout and thus avoids any 'ends' showing on the right side. Good netting is easier to achieve by commencing piping in the centre of the design and working towards the outside. Always use the touch, lift and place method of piping.

Figure 122 illustrates the carrying out of netting on a runout suitable for a 20-cm (8-in) round cake. This outline may be traced straight from the book.

REMOVING THE WAXED PAPER

Removing the waxed paper from a small runout is a simple matter, but is not so with large collars. The easiest way is to keep the runout on the board and place it on a turntable. Move the runout gently until one part is over the edge of the board. Peel the paper off the runout using a downward

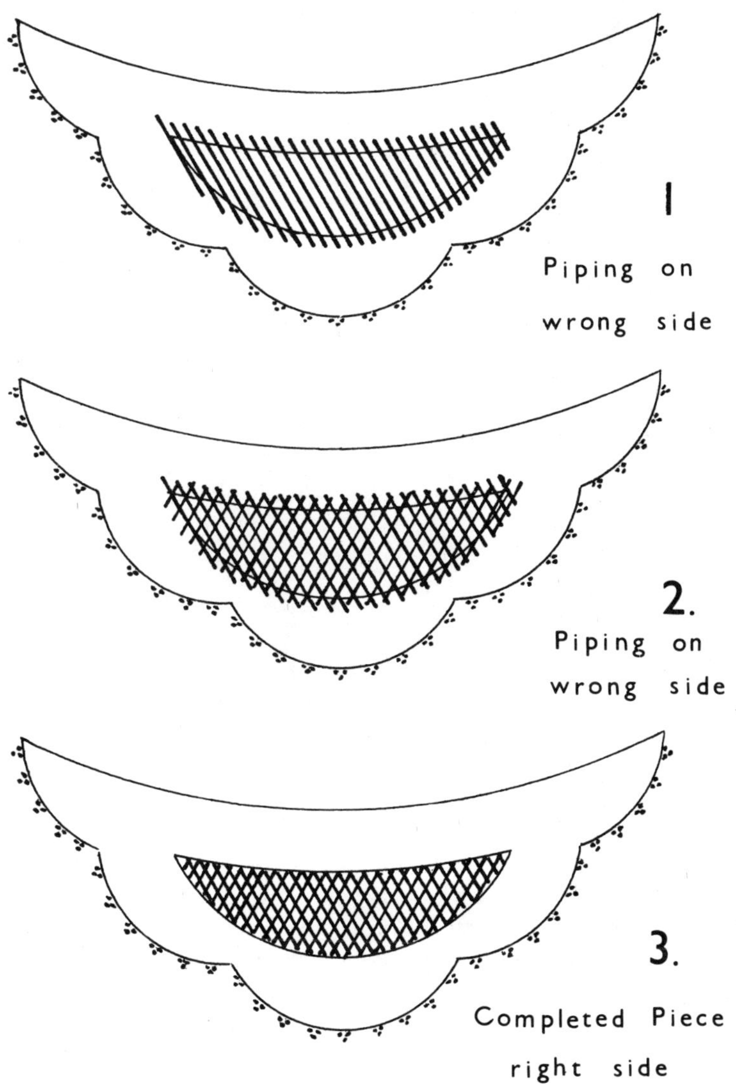

Fig. 122. Piping netting on runout pieces. Runout pieces suitable for 20-cm (8-in) cakes (six pieces on each cake).

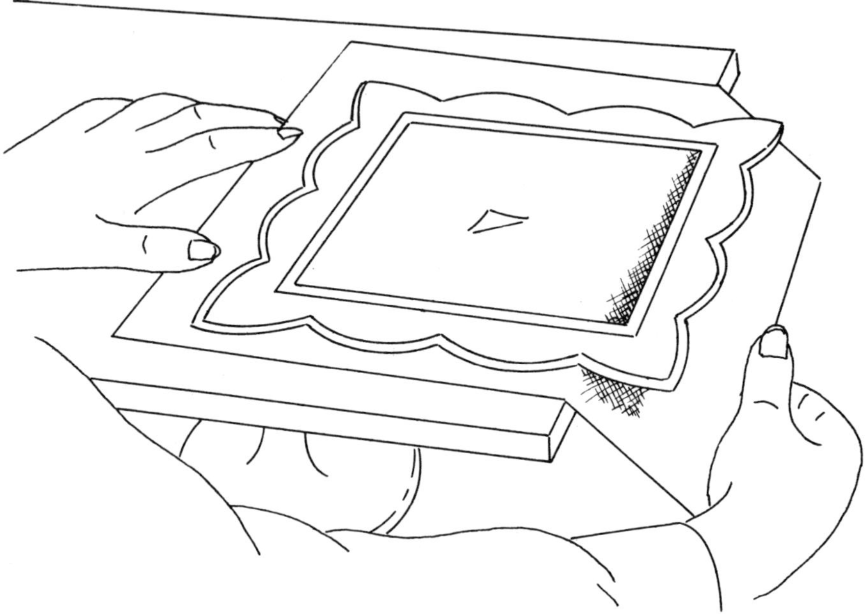

Fig. 123. Removing collar from waxed paper.

movement (Fig. 123). Turn the turntable a little and repeat until the whole runout is free.

PLACING RUNOUTS ON THE CAKE

Runout borders are stuck on to the cake edge with a little icing. When placing a collar on a cake I pipe a line of icing on to the edge of the cake with a No. 2 tube and place the collar gently on the top. For small pieces I find it easier to turn the runout over and place a little icing on the back before securing it on the cake. Care must be taken with individual pieces to obtain the correct position for the runouts and to make sure they are evenly spaced. Some form of linework or small shells may be piped inside the runouts and a small shell *underneath* the runout where it sits on the cake will result in a neat finish (Fig. 124).

ADDITIONAL DECORATION

Additional decoration can be added to runouts after they have been dried and before they have been placed on the cake. Runout holly leaves or small bells on top of filigree look very attractive and so do small piped flowers.

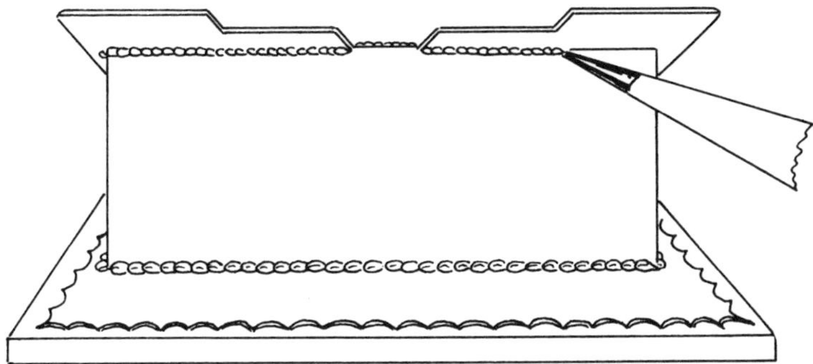

Fig. 124. Piping underneath top border runout.

Fig. 125. Additional decoration to runout collar.

Figure 125 shows a collar with runout fives placed on top of the filigree linework.

Designs for Runout Borders

Designs for collars and pieces that may be traced from the book are given in Figs. 126–143. Some show an edging in order to give a complete picture. This edging would, of course, not be piped until after the runout had dried.

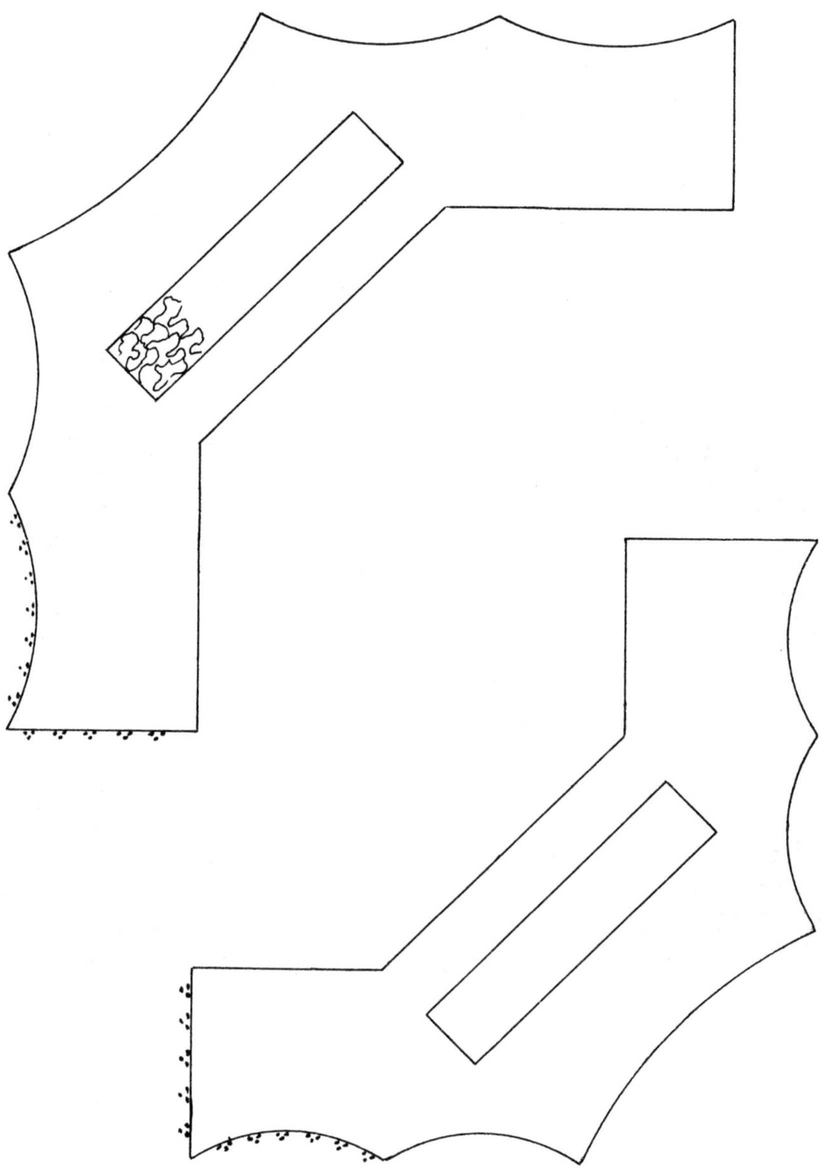

Fig. 126. Corner pieces for 15-cm (6-in) and 13-cm (5-in) square cakes.

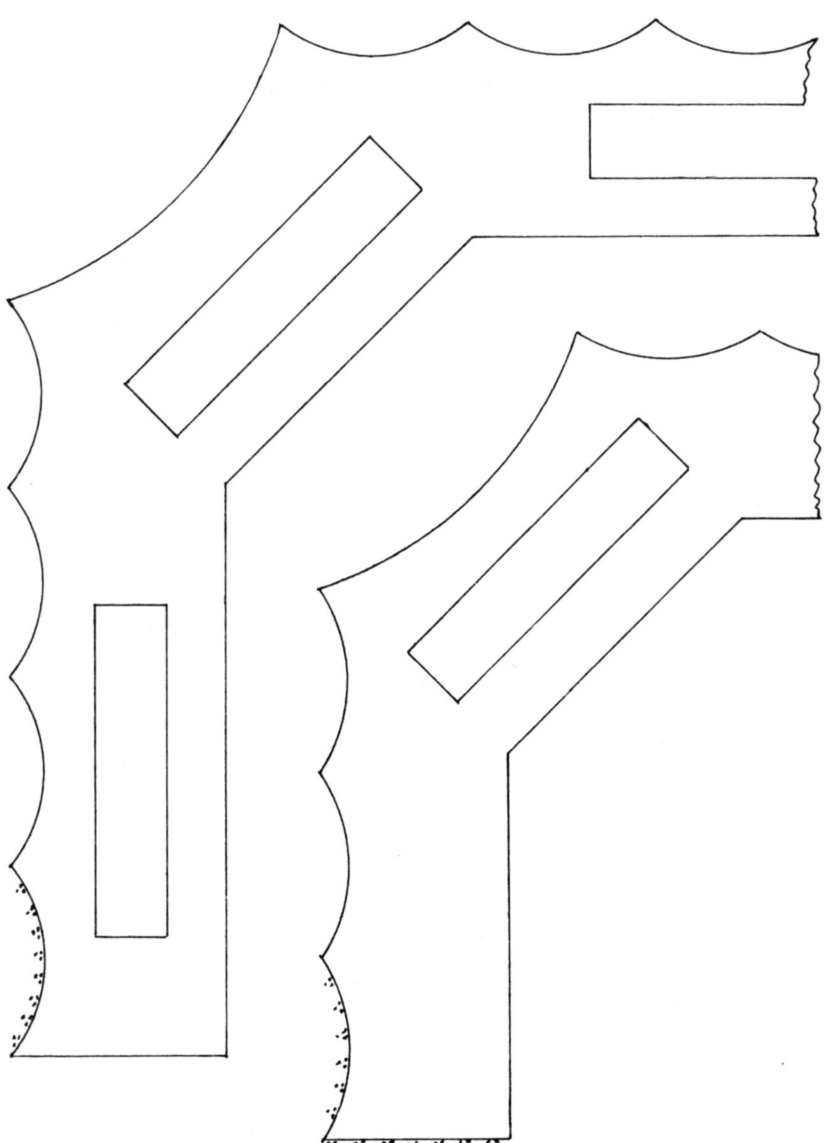

Fig. 127. Corner pieces for 23-cm (9-in) and 18-cm (7-in) square cakes.

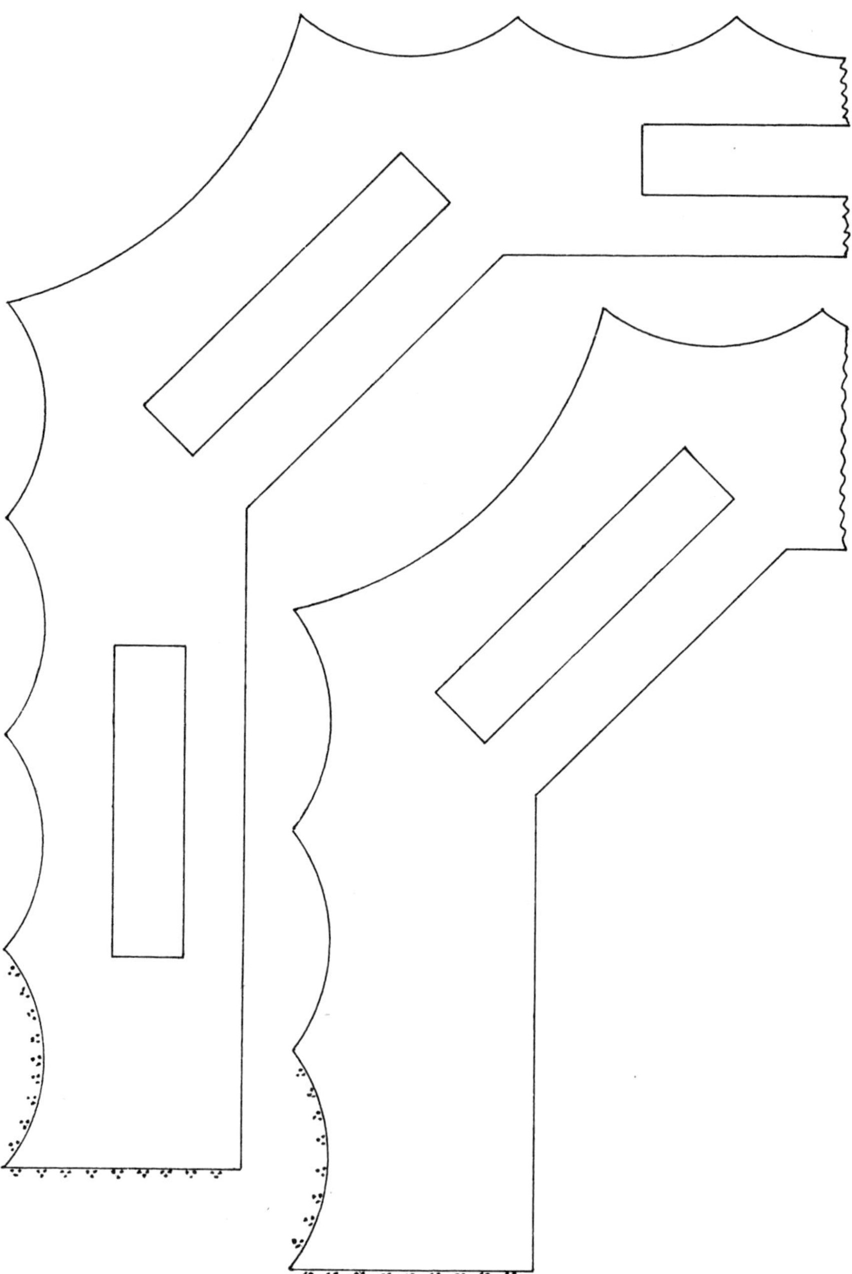

Fig. 128. Corner pieces for 25-cm (10-in) and 20-cm (8-in) square cakes.

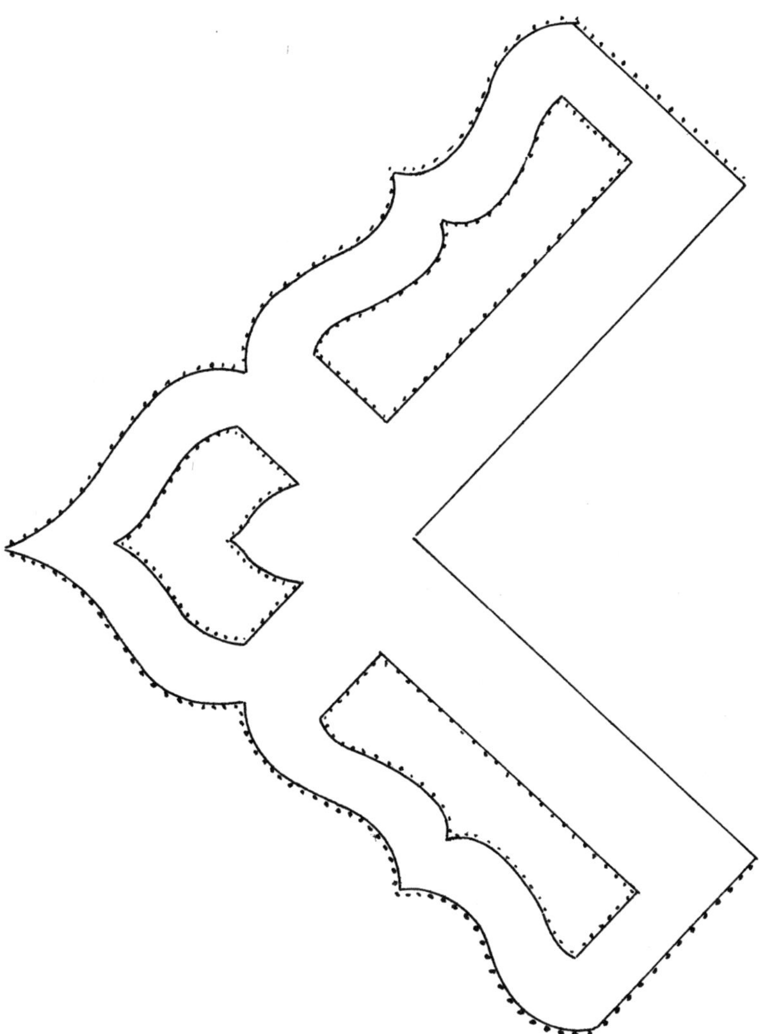

Fig. 129. Corner piece for a 15-cm (6-in) square cake.

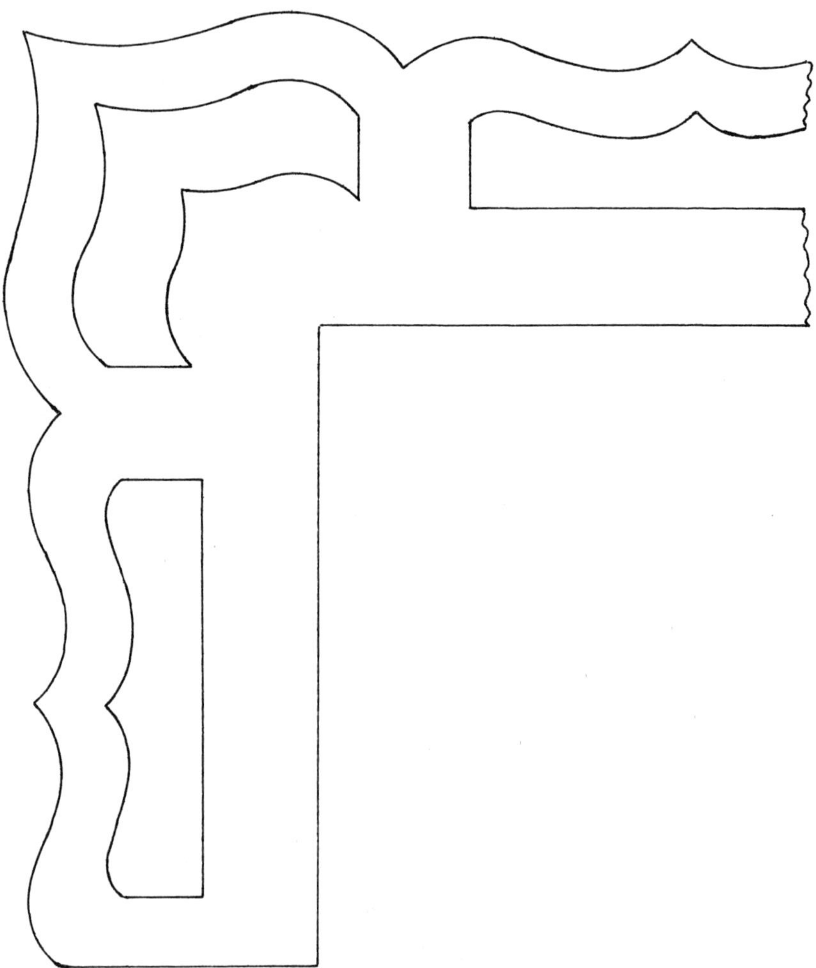

Fig. 130. Corner piece for a 20-cm (8-in) square cake.

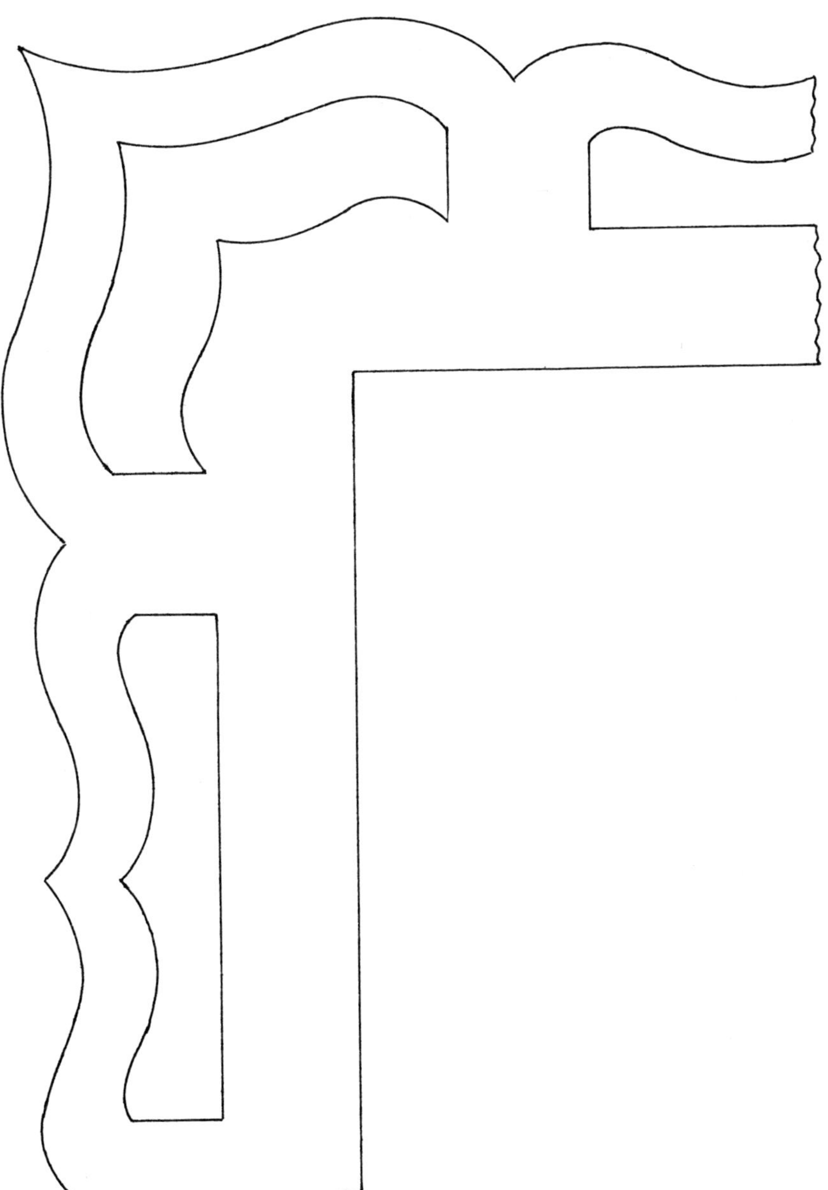

Fig. 131. Corner piece for a 25-cm (10-in) square cake.

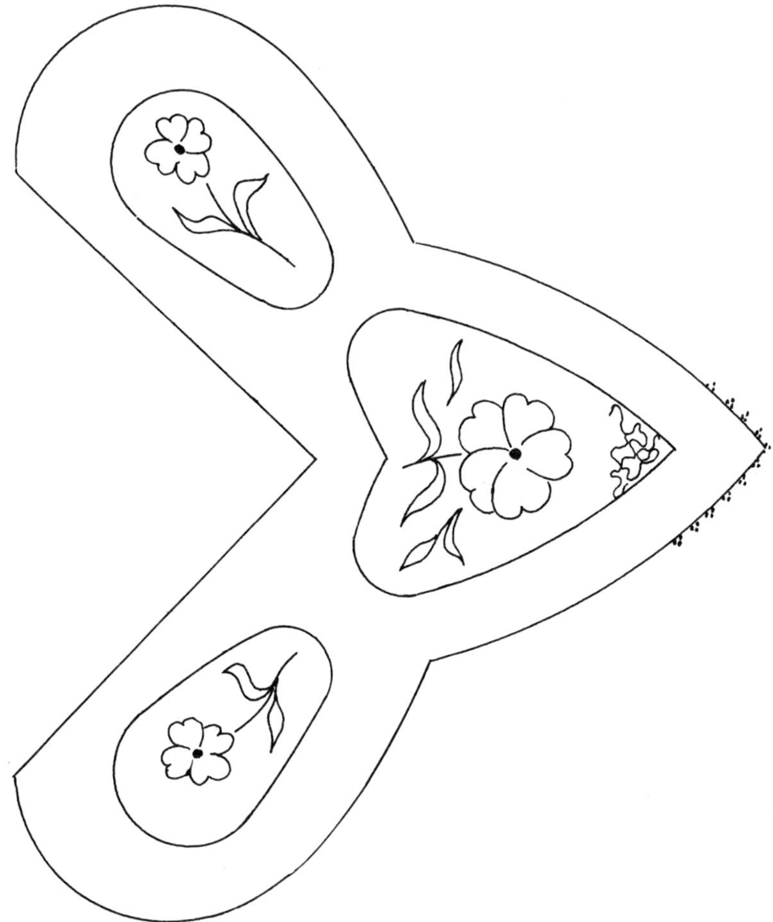

Fig. 132. Corner piece for a 15-cm (6-in) square cake.

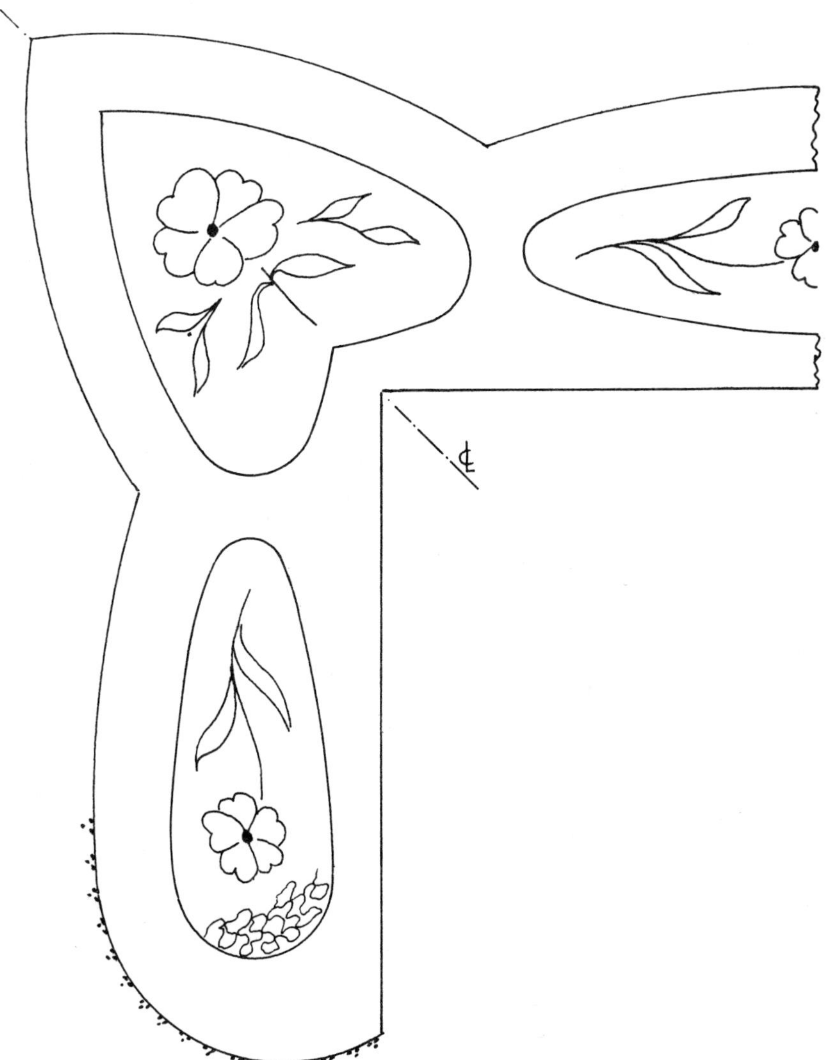

Fig. 133. Corner piece for a 20-cm (8-in) square cake.

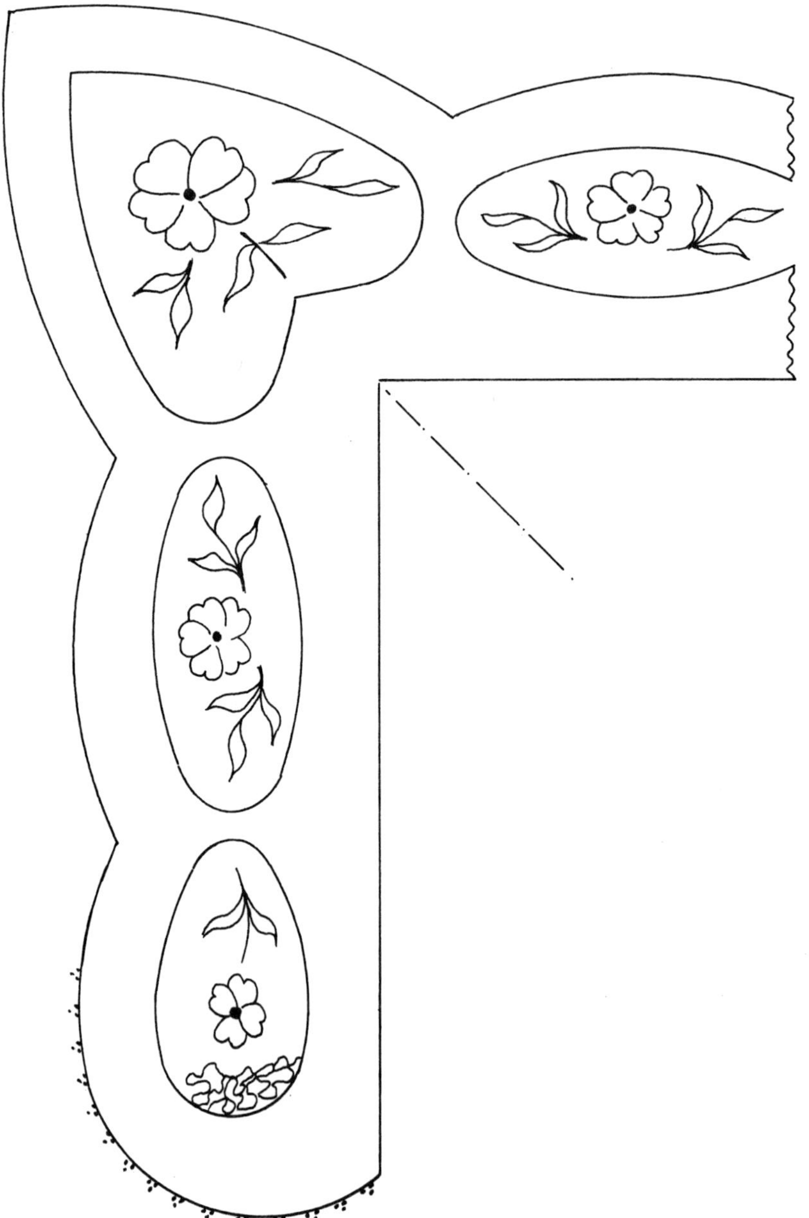

Fig. 134. Corner piece for a 25-cm (10-in) square cake.

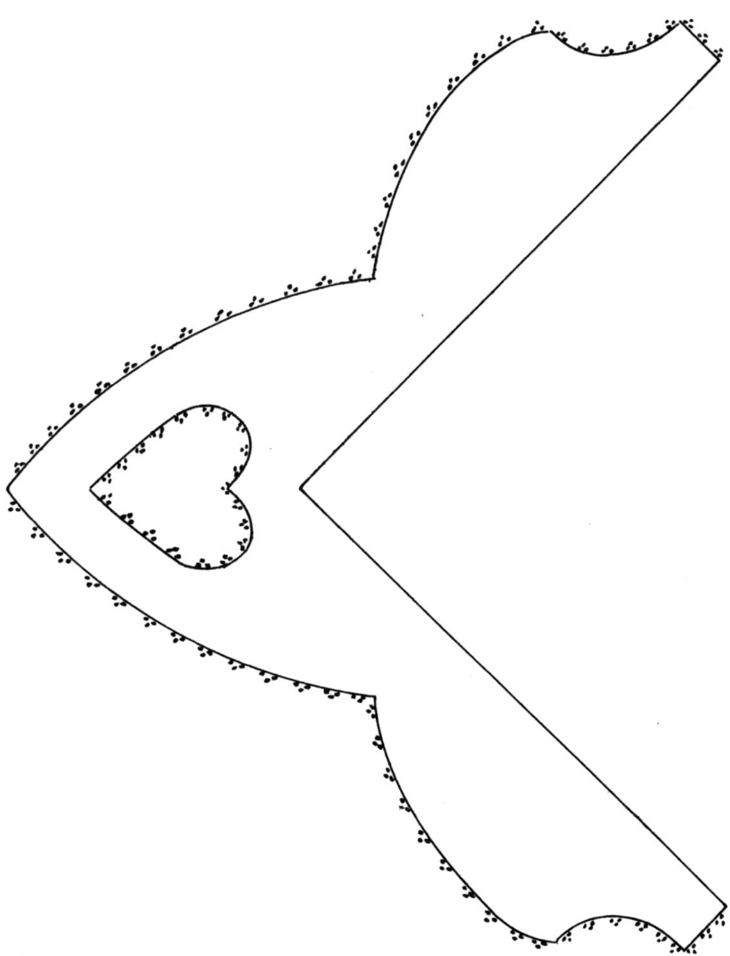

Fig. 135. Corner piece for an 18-cm (7-in) square cake.

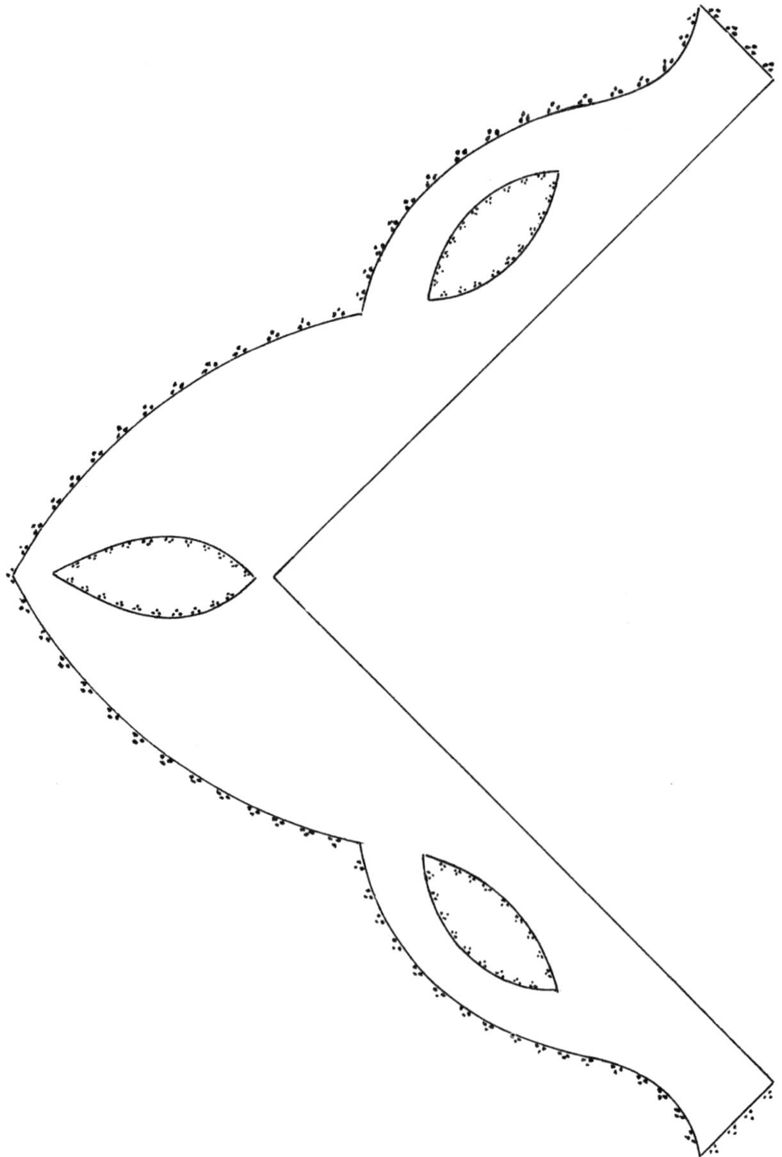

Fig. 136. Corner piece for a 20-cm (8-in) square cake.

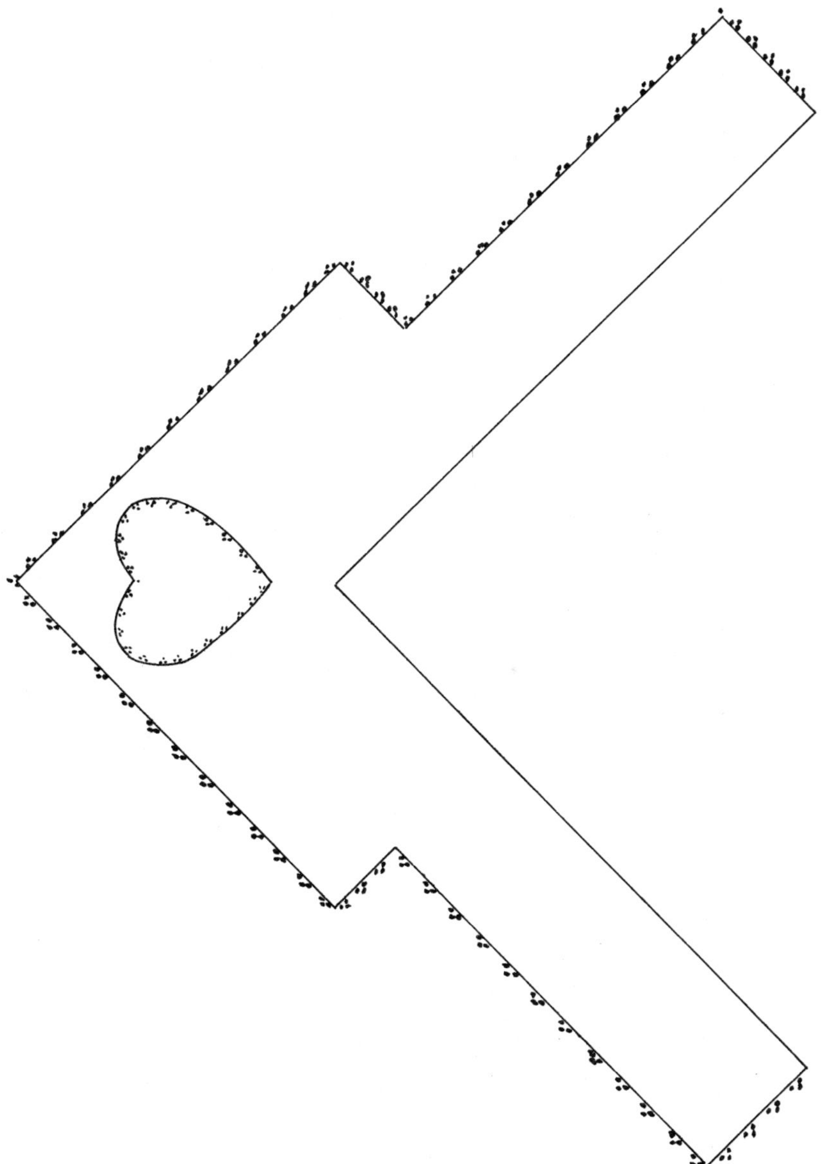

Fig. 137. Corner piece for a 20-cm (8-in) square cake.

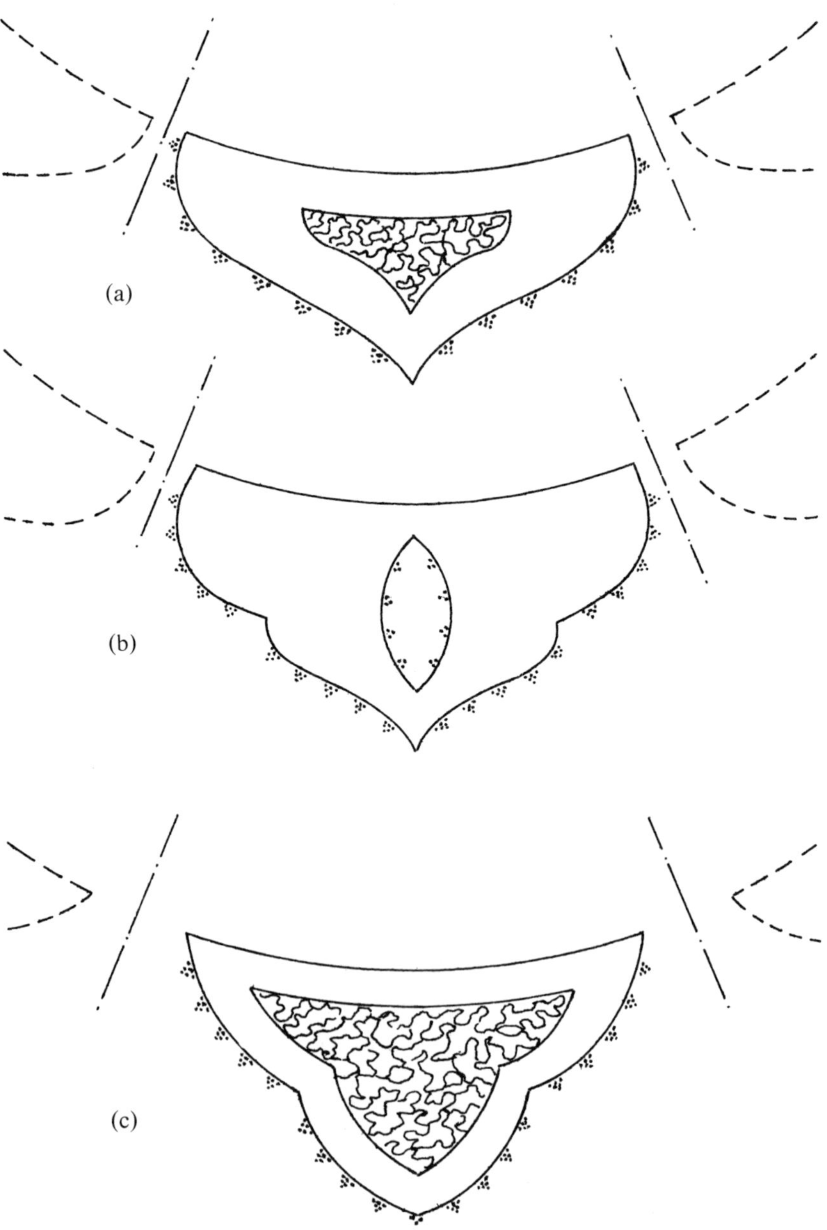

Fig. 138. (a) and (b) Eight pieces on an 18-cm (7-in) round cake. (c) Eight pieces on a 20-cm (8-in) round cake.

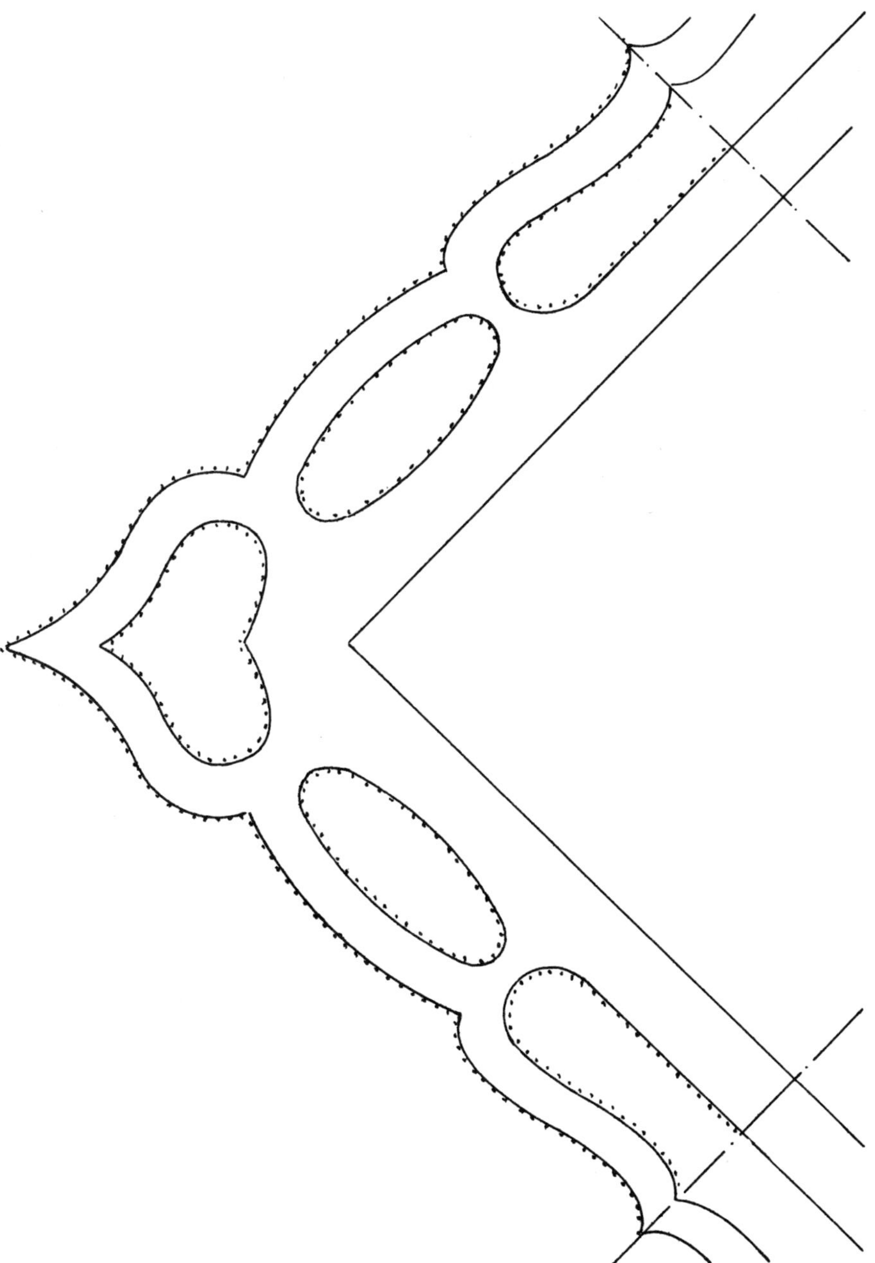

Fig. 139. An 18-cm (7-in) collar (square).

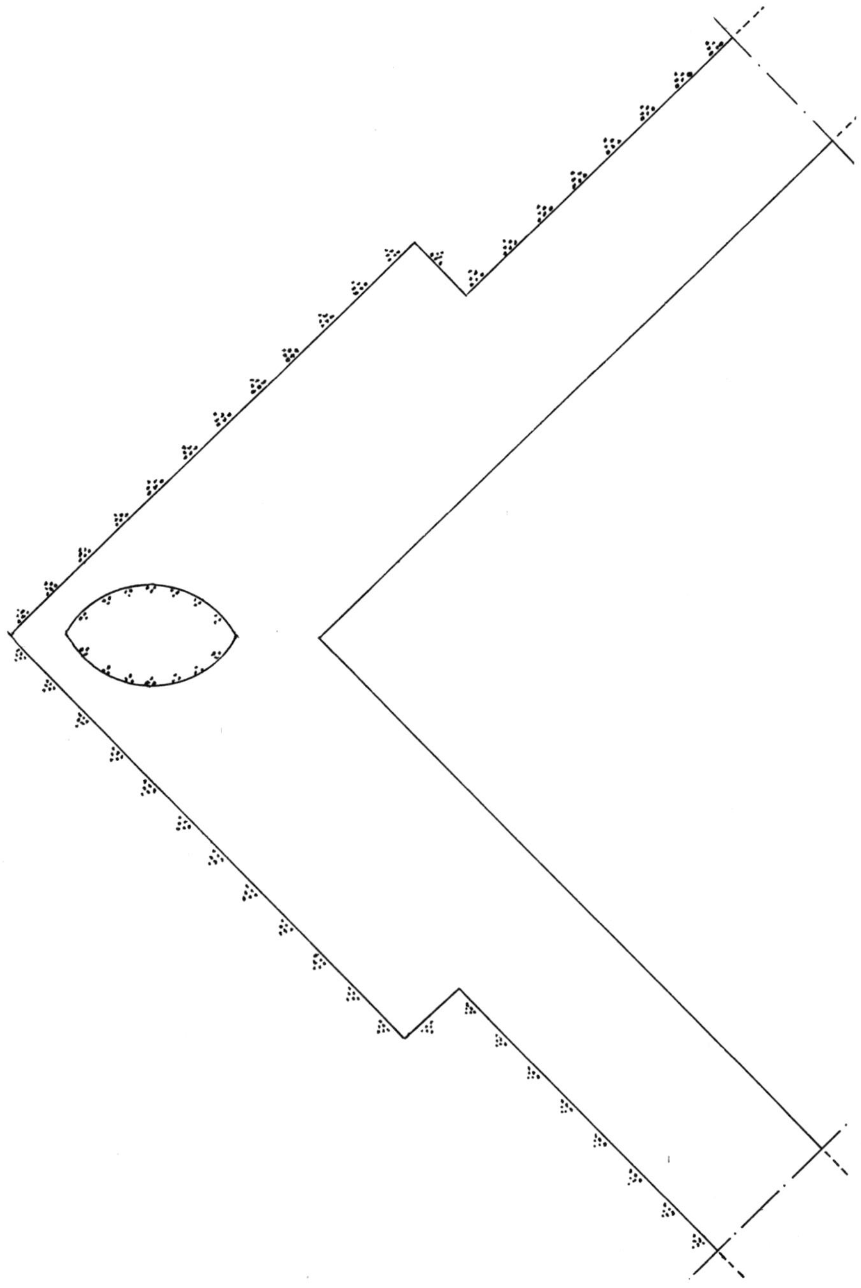

Fig. 140. A 20-cm (8-in) collar (square).

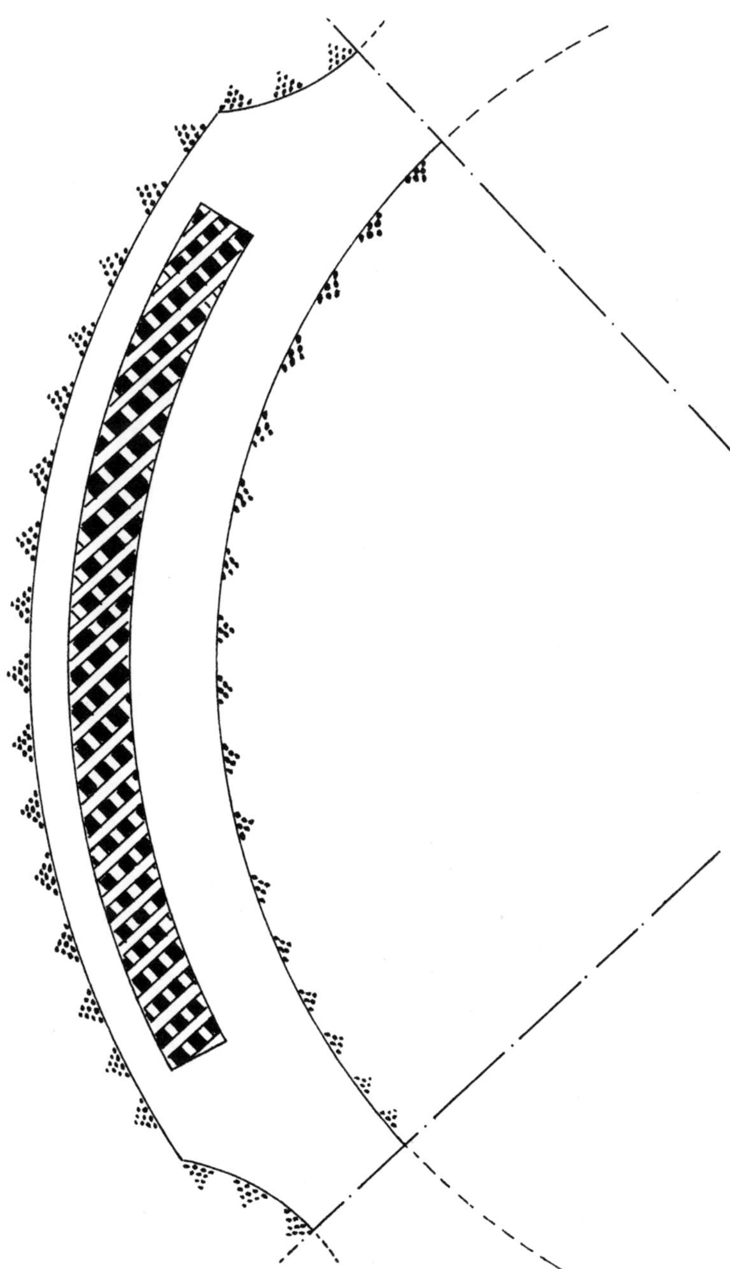

Fig. 141. A 20-cm (8-in) collar (round).

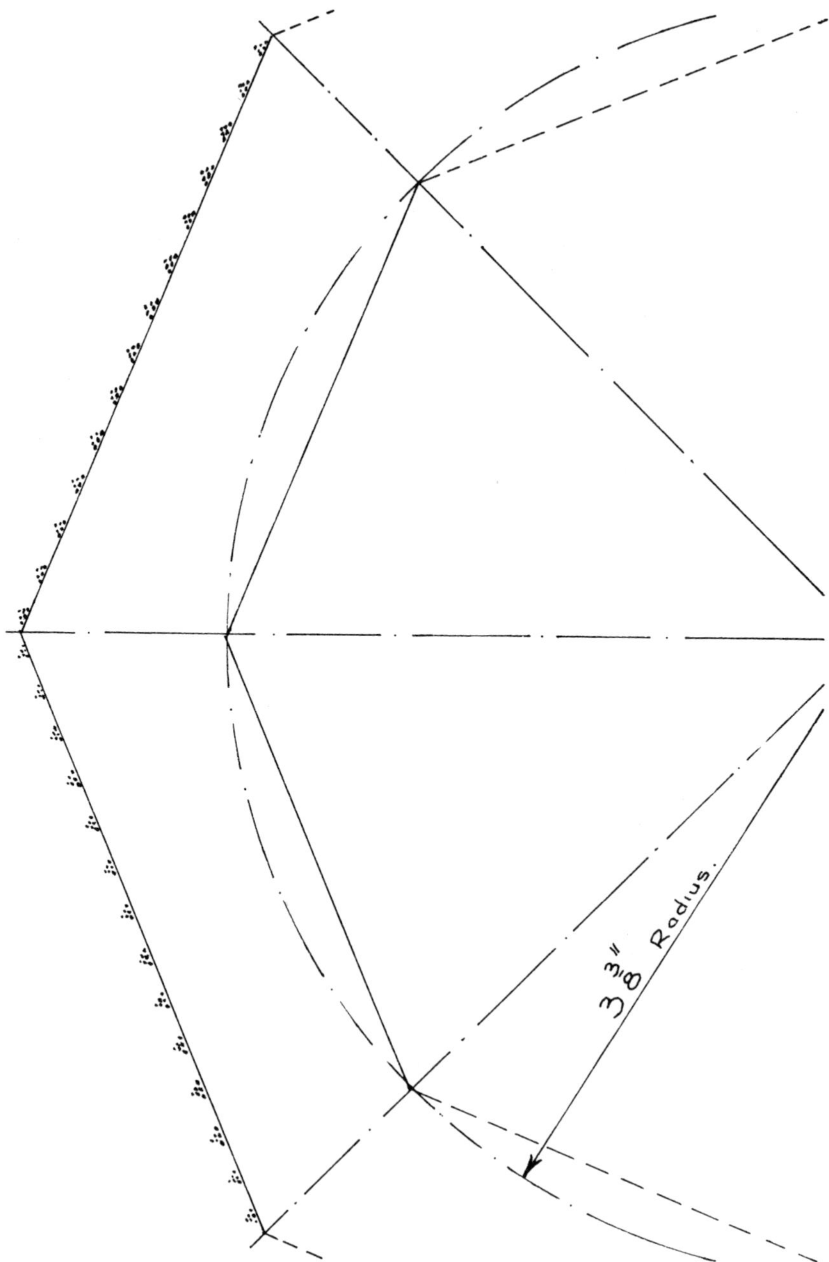

Fig. 142. An 18-cm (7-in) collar (round).

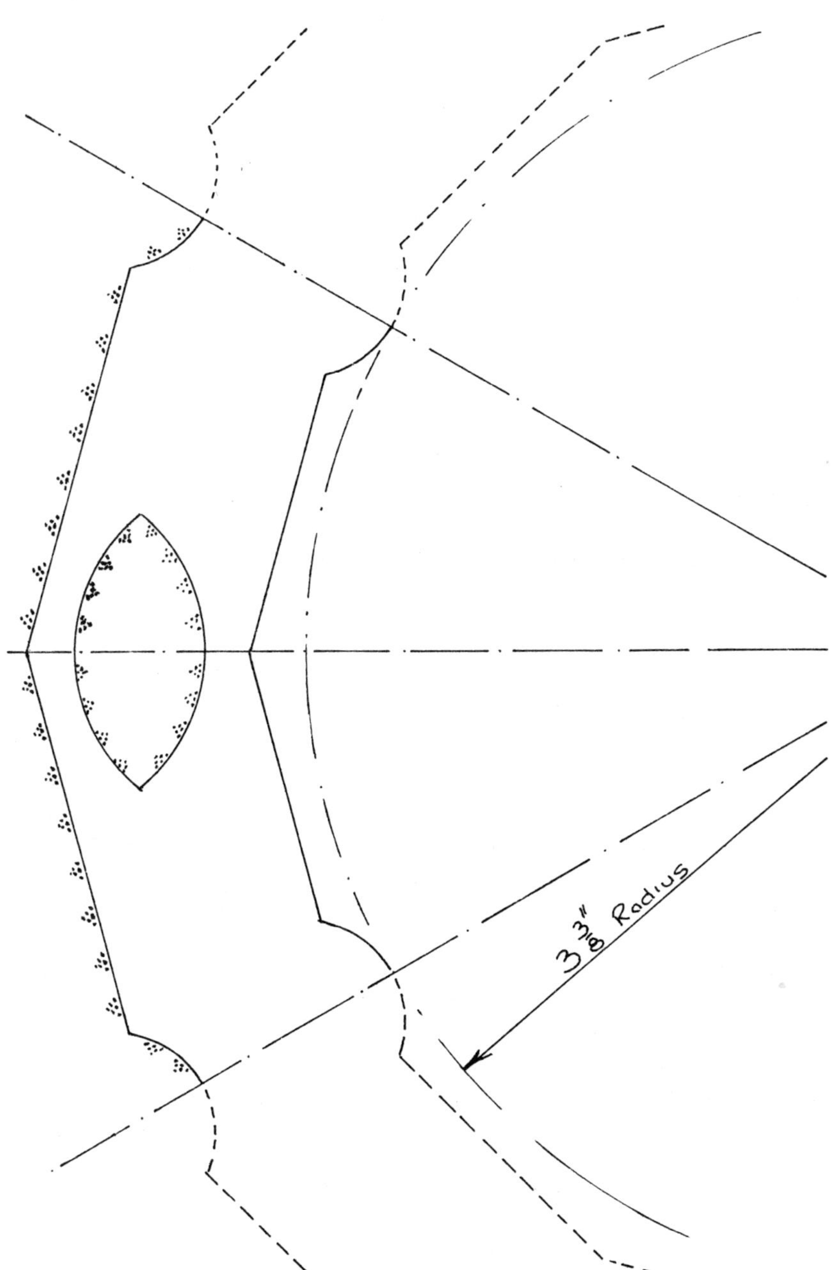

Fig. 143. A 20-cm (8-in) collar (round).

Chapter 15

Finished Cakes

All the designs required to execute the cakes illustrated in this chapter are to be found in this book. Every aspect of piping used has been covered and a brief description is given to enable them to be easily reproduced.

Christening Cake (Figs. 144 and 145)

Tubes used: Nos. 3, 2, 1 and 0.

Colour: Pale pink.

Base decoration: The bottom border was flooded before the rest of the cake was decorated. This is a plain flooded border (Figs. 43 and 44, Chapter 7) overpiped, when dry, with filigree linework from a No. 0 tube. The shell border on top of the flooding was made with a No. 3 tube (Fig. 33, Chapter 6) and the edging is a series of small bulbs (Fig. 31(c), Chapter 6) executed with a No. 0 tube.

Top decoration: The runout stork is white with the exception of the beak which is deep pink. The eye was painted after the runout had dried and the legs were piped directly on the cake with a No. 0 tube using brown icing.

The lettering is a combination of runout and direct piping. The initials were runout on waxed paper in deep pink and placed on the cake when dry. The remainder of the lettering was piped in pale pink using a No. 2 tube and overpiped in deep pink with a No. 1 tube.

The runout corner pieces can be found in Fig. 137, Chapter 14, and in this case the hearts contain filigree linework. A No. 3 shell border was piped inside and underneath the runout corner pieces.

Side decoration: White and pink runout teddy bears and rabbits are on

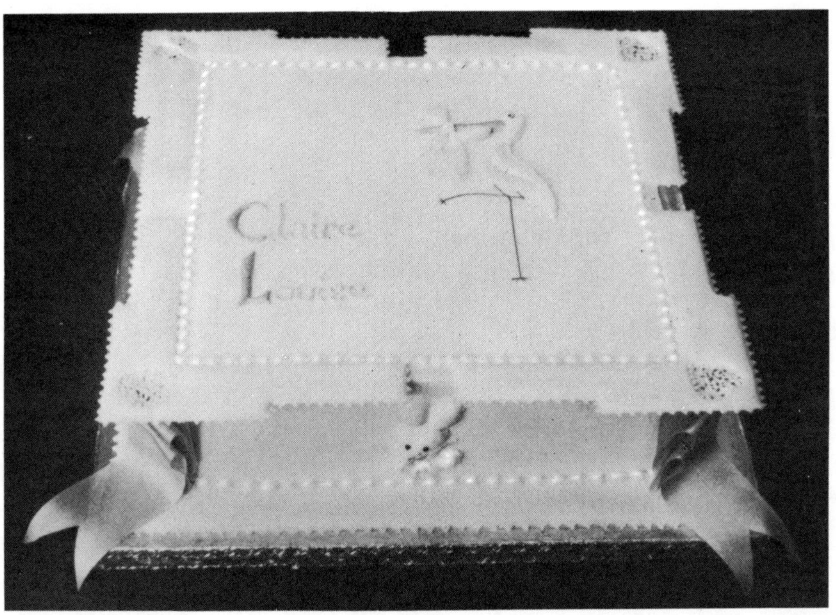

Fig. 144. Christening cake.

Fig. 145. Christening cake.

alternate sides of the cake and deep pink looped ribbons form the corner decoration.

Fifth Birthday Cake (Figs. 146 and 147)

Tubes used: Nos. 3, 2, 1 and 0.

Colour: Pale turquoise.

Base decoration: The bottom border was flooded to match the top collar with the aid of a template and this was done before the rest of the cake was decorated. When dry, a No. 3 shell border was piped and an edging formed by a series of bulbs with a No. 0 tube.

Top decoration: The collar for this cake can be found in Fig. 142, Chapter 14. The runout plaque is a deeper shade of turquoise and contains runout figures which were assembled after the plaque had dried but before it was placed on the cake. A little additional piping was made in the form of grass and flowers (Fig. 31, Chapter 6) with No. 0 tubes. The edging to the plaque was piped with a No. 0 tube in deep turquoise after the plaque had been secured to the cake.

No. 3 and No. 2 linework was piped inside the collar and No. 3 shell underneath.

Fig. 146. Fifth birthday cake.

Fig. 147. Fifth birthday cake.

Side decoration: The white lambs were piped on waxed paper and placed on the cake when dry. Even spacing was obtained by placing one underneath each section of the top runout border. Grass and flowers similar to those on the plaque were piped directly on the side of the cake using bright colours and No. 0 tubes.

Seventh Birthday Cake (Fig. 148)

Tubes used: Nos. 44, 3, 2, 1 and 0.

Colour: White.

Top decoration: The number seven was painted on the balloons before the runouts were placed on the cake. The strings were piped directly on to the cake with brown icing using a No. 0 tube.

The top of the cake was divided into twelve sections and a single 'S' scroll border piped with a No. 44 tube. The overpiping is the same as that described in Fig. 37, Chapter 7, for the double 'S' scroll border. Linework underneath the border was made with No. 3 and No. 2 tubes.

Side decoration: Six evenly-spaced coloured balloons form the side decoration. The strings were piped directly on to the cake with a No. 0 tube.

Fig. 148. Seventh birthday cake.

Base decoration: This shell border was outlined with curved linework using No. 3 and No. 2 tubes.

Girl's Birthday Cake (Fig. 149)

Tubes used: Nos. 3, 2, 1 and 0.

Colour: White.

Base decoration: A plain flooded border executed before the commencement of any further decoration. A No. 3 shell border and a No. 0 edging complete the bottom border.

Top decoration: The tree was piped directly on to the cake with a No. 0 tube and brown icing before the runout figures were assembled. Grass and foliage were applied with a paint brush, using green colouring, prior to flowers and blossom being piped with No. 0 tubes in bright colours (see p. 108).

The runout pieces can be found in Fig. 136, Chapter 14, and the linework inside was made with No. 3 and No. 2 tubes and a No. 3 shell was piped underneath the runout border.

Fig. 149. Girl's birthday cake. © *1970 Hallmark Cards Inc.*

Side decoration: plaques form the side decoration and the corners are decorated with looped ribbons.

Boy's Birthday Cake (Figs. 150 and 151)

Tubes used: Nos. 3, 1 and 0.

Colour: White.

Base decoration: Border flooded to match the outline of the top runout border and edged with single bulbs using a No. 0 tube.

Top decoration: The runout galleon was assembled on the cake when dry and the rigging was piped directly on to the cake using a No. 0 tube with brown icing. The runout lettering was assembled on the cake with the aid of a template (Fig. 49, Chapter 8).

Fig. 150. Boy's birthday cake.

Fig. 151. Boy's birthday cake.

The runout pieces can be found in Fig. 130, Chapter 14. The inside linework is a No. 3 shell and a similar border was piped underneath the runout corner pieces.

Side decoration: White runout monograms and piped corner pieces (Fig. 70, Chapter 11) form the side decoration.

Crinoline Lady Cake (Fig. 152)

Tubes used: Nos. 3, 2, 1 and 0.
Colour: Pale lemon.
Base decoration: The bottom border was flooded and edged with bulbs

Fig. 152. Crinoline lady cake.

using a No. 0 tube. A border on top of the flooding was executed with a No. 3 tube.

Side decoration: Although it is not necessary to divide the cake for the top border, a template was placed on the cake and eight dots made equal distance apart in order that the side decoration would be evenly spaced. The vases were placed in line with the dots, and lines of small bulbs in deep blue icing were piped with a No. 0 tube to represent flowers.

Top decoration: The tree was piped on the cake before the commencement of further decoration. The same No. 0 tube with brown icing was then used to form the crazy paving stones. Grass in between and around the stones and foliage on the tree was achieved with the aid of a paint brush and green colouring. A No. 0 tube with deep yellow icing was used to pipe the laburnum on the tree in clusters of small dots.

The crinoline lady and the sundial were affixed to the cake and more flowers piped at the base of the tree in deep blue and similar flowers piped in the hand with a No. 0 tube. A No. 0 tube with green icing was also used to add foliage to the flowers. Curls underneath the hat were added with the brown icing.

The top border is a combined 'S' and 'C' scroll (Fig. 31, Chapter 6 and Fig. 36, Chapter 7) executed with a No. 3 tube. The border was edged with curves using tubes Nos. 3 and 2.

Eighteenth Birthday Cake (Fig. 153)

Tubes used: Nos. 3, 1 and 0.

Colour: Pale lemon.

Base decoration: The bottom border was flooded and edged with bulbs using a No. 0 tube. A shell border on top of the flooding was executed with a No. 3 tube.

Top decoration: The number eighteen, butterflies, leaves and the corner runout pieces (Fig. 128) were all runout in pale-lemon icing. When dry, the butterflies, leaves and the corners of the runout pieces were decorated with very small flowers (Fig. 31(c), Chapter 6) using No. 0 tubes with blue and mauve icing. Very small bulbs of green icing were also added.

The number eighteen was placed on the cake before the remainder of the runouts were assembled. Linework inside the top runout border is a combined 'S' and 'C' scroll made with a No. 3 tube, and a No. 3 shell was piped underneath.

Fig. 153. Eighteenth birthday cake.

Side decoration: Runout ballet shoes in pale lemon, partially painted with silver, when dry, form the side decoration. The pale-lemon looped ribbons were decorated with small flowers similar to those on the top runouts.

Twenty-first Birthday Cake (Fig. 154)

Tubes used: Nos. 44, 3, 2 and 1.

Colour: Pale pink.

Top decoration: Before assembling the pink marzipan roses a line was drawn across the cake with a No. 0 tube and brown icing. Smaller lines branching off from the first were then made, the tube lightly touching the surface whilst this took place.

The roses were assembled to form a spray and the leaves placed around them. Roses and leaves were stuck to the cake with a little icing when the correct positioning had been achieved. The number twenty-one was affixed to the cake before the border was piped.

Fig. 154. Twenty-first birthday cake.

Each side of the cake was divided into three sections before the commencement of the rope border (Fig. 38, Chapter 7). The final overpiping with a No. 1 tube is deep pink to contrast with the pale-pink coating and previous piping.

Side decoration: A pale-pink vase and two small pink butterflies form part of each side decoration. Additional linework with a No. 0 tube completes the ornamentation. Pale-pink looped ribbons were attached, with icing, to each corner.

Base decoration: The bottom border matches the top border and was outlined with curves using No. 3 and No. 2 tubes.

Father Christmas Christmas Cake (Fig. 155)

Tubes used: Nos. 44, 1 and 0.

Colour: White.

Base decoration: The bottom border was flooded and edged with bulbs from a No. 0 tube. A shell border on top of the flooding was executed with a No. 44 tube.

Side decoration: Although the top of the cake does not need to be divided for the piped border, eight divisions can usefully be made so that the red

Fig. 155. Father Christmas Christmas cake.

Christmas stockings can be placed on the side of the cake directly below the marks. The small bulbs of icing on the top of the cake were removed before the border was piped.

Top decoration: This runout figure should be colourful and so in addition to the red cloak and hood, the sack was flooded green. The chimney and glove are brown and additional brown painting on the chimney signifies the bricks.

The top border is a No. 44 shell as shown in Fig..33, Chapter 6, and Fig. 35, Chapter 7.

Three Wise Men Christmas Cake (Fig. 156)

Tubes used: Nos. 3, 2, 1 and 0.

Colour: White.

Base decoration: This is a plain flooded border with a No. 3 shell border on top of the flooding and a bulb edging executed with a No. 0 tube.

Top decoration: The runout figures should be made as colourful as possible and additional painting and piping applied after the runouts have dried. They were placed on the cake before the runout collar was secured.

The collar can be found in Fig. 140, Chapter 14, and inside linework was

Fig. 156. Three Wise Men Christmas cake.

carried out with No. 3 and No. 2 tubes. A shell border was piped underneath the collar with a No. 3 tube.

Side decoration: A red satin ribbon with a sewn bow completes the decoration.

Mary and Joseph Christmas Cake (Fig. 157)

Tubes used: Nos. 13, 3, 2, 1 and 0.

Colour: White.

Base decoration: A plain flooded border overpiped, when dry, with filigree linework using a No. 0 tube; a No. 3 shell border on top of the flooding and an edging of small bulbs using a No. 0 tube.

Top decoration: The soft sugar border was carried out (Figs. 40 and 41, Chapter 7) and left to dry before the figures were placed in the centre of the cake. The crook was piped directly on to the cake with a No. 0 tube and brown icing. Linework underneath the shell border was made with tubes Nos. 3, 2 and 1. The small bulbs inside the flooded border match those on

Fig. 157. Mary and Joseph Christmas cake.

the outside of the bottom border. No. 0 filigree linework on top of the soft sugar border was carried out when the flooding was absolutely dry.

Side decoration: By following the pattern on the top of the cake it is easy to space the angels evenly around the side. The angel wings were made separately and painted gold whilst still on the waxed paper. The hair was flooded pale yellow and the rest of the angel was flooded white. When dry, but before being lifted from the waxed paper, the crown was painted gold and the hair streaked lightly with yellow colouring.

After assembling the angels, the wings were placed on either side with a little icing. It is necessary to hold them in place for a few moments until they are firmly attached to the side of the cake.

Nativity Christmas Cake (Fig. 158)

Tubes used: Nos. 3, 1 and 0.
Colour: White.

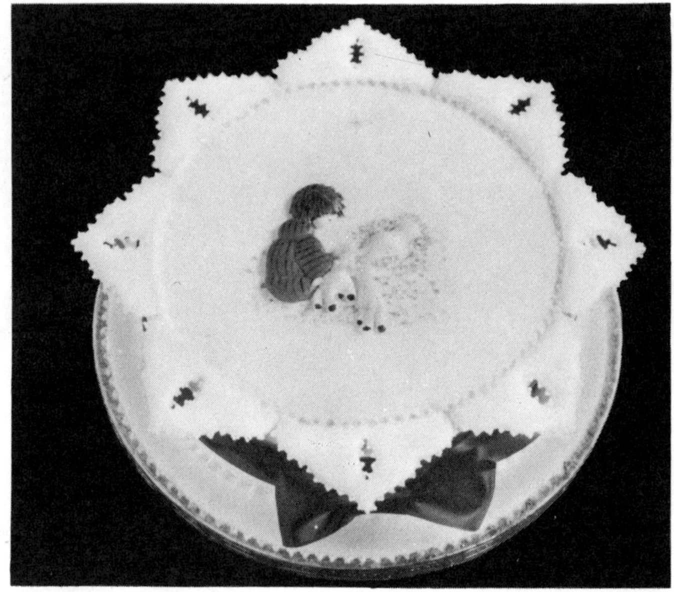

Fig. 158. Nativity Christmas cake.

Base decoration: The bottom border was flooded and edged with small bulbs using a No. 0 tube. A shell border on top of the flooding was executed with a No. 3 tube.

Top decoration: Before the runout figures were placed on the cake, straw was painted with a fine paint brush. The yellow star was also painted with a fine paint brush.

The runout border pieces can be found in Fig. 138, Chapter 14, and the inside edging is the same series of No. 0 bulbs carried out on the edge of the runout pieces and the flooded bottom border. A No. 3 shell border was piped underneath the runout pieces.

Side decoration: A red satin ribbon with a sewn bow forms the side decoration.

Round Wedding Cake (Figs. 159–161)

Tubes used: Nos. 44, 3, 2, 1 and 0.

Colour: White.

General comments: There should be no difficulty in icing a tiered cake provided the cakes are level and well coated.

The size of the cakes are 15 cm (6 in), 20 cm (8 in) and 25 cm (10 in), and are placed on 20 cm (8 in), 25 cm (10 in) and 33 cm (13 in) boards. Eight round pillars are required and they must be evenly spaced when placed on the cakes.

Side decorations: A template is required for the sides of the cakes and with the exception of the small runouts, the side piping is the same on each cake (Fig. 160). Where side decorations are to be done in this manner they should be completed *before* the bottom border is flooded.

To make a template, measure the exact length around the cake and cut a piece of paper to suit. Fold the paper into the desired number of sections (six for the 15- and 20-cm cakes and eight for the 25-cm cake) and cut out a curve. Open out the paper to form a series of scallops and place around the cake, holding it in position with a little icing. Leave the paper on the cake until enough of the pattern has been piped to be able to provide an accurate design (Fig. 159).

Pipe the designs on the sides in white icing using a No. 0 tube, as shown in Fig. 160. The piping was made by lightly touching the surface of the cake. The top tier has additional decoration in the form of runout hearts whilst the middle tier is adorned with bells and the bottom tier birds.

Base decorations: The bottom boards were flooded and edged with bulbs from a No. 0 tube. The flooding was overpiped with filigree linework from a No. 0 tube. The shell border on top of the flooding was made with a No. 3 tube.

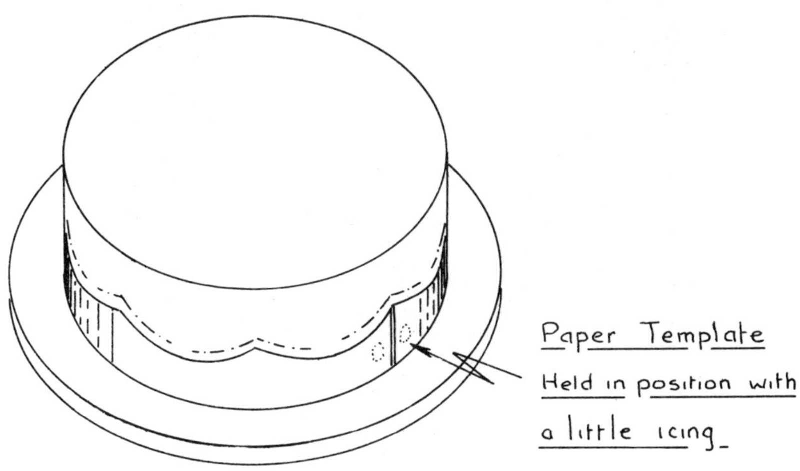

Fig. 159. Template for side of round cake.

Fig. 160. Close-up of side piping on wedding cake.

Fig. 161. Three-tier round wedding cake.

Top decorations: The central decoration on the bottom two tiers is a marguerite and on the top tier a water lily. A rope border as shown in Fig. 38, Chapter 7, and underpiping with tubes Nos. 3 and 2 completes the design (Fig. 161).

Square Wedding Cake (Fig. 162)

Tubes used: Nos. 3, 2, 1 and 0.
Colour: White.
General comments: A 15-cm (6-in) and a 25-cm (10-in) cake were placed on 25-cm (10-in) and 35-cm (14-in) boards, respectively. Both tiers were

Fig. 162. Two-tier square wedding cake.

decorated in the same way except that a marguerite was used in the centre of the bottom tier. Four square pillars are required and the top ornament is a vase of flowers.

Base decorations: The bottom borders were flooded (with the aid of templates) to match the outline of the top runout pieces. Filigree linework with a No. 0 tube was piped on top when the icing was dry. An edging of small bulbs was made around the borders and a No. 3 shell on top of the borders completes the base decorations.

Top decorations: The marguerite was assembled in the centre of the bottom tier and stamens in the centre were piped in white with a No. 0 tube. When dry, the stamens were lightly touched with silver paint.

The runout corner pieces are to be found in Figs. 132 and 134, Chapter 14. The flowers and leaves were piped inside the pieces with slightly softened white icing in a No. 1 tube. When dry they were painted silver and the outlines of the runouts were piped with a No. 1 tube. The filigree was added and finally the outlines were flooded in the usual way.

Because silver was used the design had to be piped in white and then painted. It is easier to paint the flowers, etc. before the filigree is piped, thus avoiding the paint touching another part of the icing. If coloured flowers and leaves instead of silver ones are being done, there is no need to let the icing completely dry before the filigree linework is piped.

The No. 3 and No. 2 linework inside the runout pieces should be carried out before the butterflies are assembled.

Side decorations: Bells and monograms form alternate decorations on the sides of the cakes. The white monograms were painted silver whilst still attached to the waxed paper. This way any surplus paint was left on the paper when the monogram was placed on the cake.

The depths of the sides of the cakes were measured before the drawings for the piped corner pieces were made. They were attached to the cake with a little icing which was made smooth with the aid of a paint brush.

Silver Wedding Cake (Fig. 163)

Tubes used: Nos. 3, 2, 1 and 0.

Colour: White.

Base decoration: The bottom border was runout to match the top collar and overpiped with No. 0 filigree linework when dry. A No. 3 shell and an edging with a No. 0 tube complete the design.

Top decoration: The white plaque was decorated with a spray of heather piped directly on to the plaque with brown icing using a No. 0 tube. Small

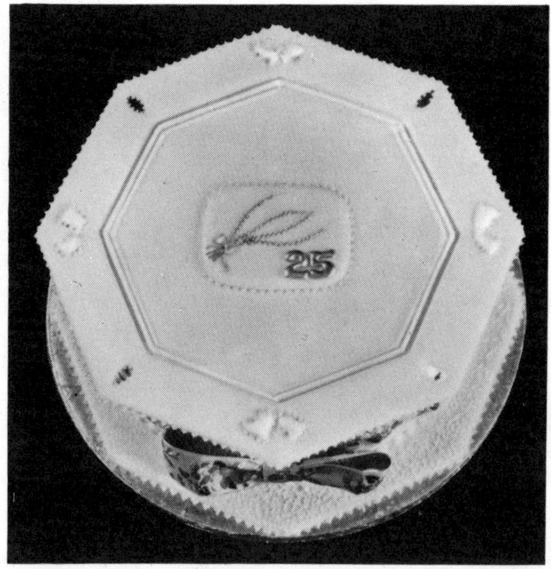

Fig. 163. Silver wedding cake.

bulbs of purple and very tiny dots of green were applied to the stem with a No. 0 tube and a small bow piped also with a No. 0 tube.

The number twenty-five was runout on waxed paper and painted, when dry, with silver before being taken from the paper and placed on to the plaque. The No. 0 edging to the plaque was piped after it had been affixed to the cake.

The plain collar in Fig. 142, Chapter 14, was altered slightly to include small insets and runout bells. The linework inside the collar was made with No. 3 and No. 2 tubes, and a No. 3 shell border was piped underneath the collar.

Side decoration: A ribbon and a sewn bow secured with white icing.

Ruby Wedding Cake (Fig. 164)

Tubes used: Nos. 3, 2, 1 and 0.

Colour: White.

General comments: This design can be used for many occasions by placing the appropriate number in the runout heart. A pale lemon cake with

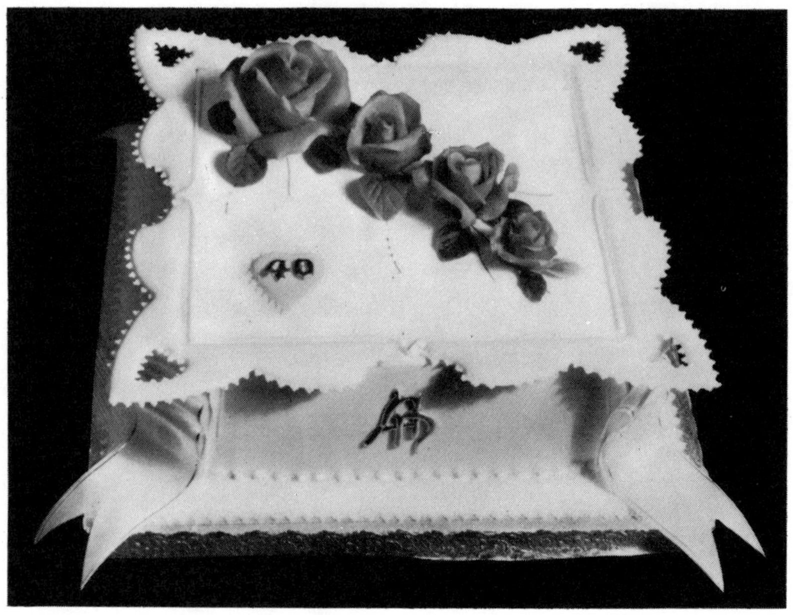

Fig. 164. Ruby wedding cake.

deep yellow roses and a gold painted number fifty placed on a yellow heart is ideal for a Golden Wedding.

Base decoration: This is a plain flooded border (Fig. 44, Chapter 7) over-piped when dry with filigree linework using a No. 0 tube. A plain shell border with a No. 3 tube was executed over the flooded border.

Top decoration: This spray of red roses was assembled in a similar way to that in Fig. 154. The runout heart contains the number forty which was placed on top of the heart after being painted silver. The heart was edged with a No. 0 tube after it had been fixed to the cake.

The runout corner pieces are to be found in Fig. 135, Chapter 14, and the linework inside the runouts was made with No. 3 and No. 2 tubes. A border underneath the runout pieces is a No. 3 shell.

Side decoration: The side decoration consists of monograms on each side and looped ribbons on each corner.

Index